Your Immortal Body of Light

by
Mitchell Earl Gibson, M.D.

Reality Press
An imprint of Reality Entertainment, Inc.

For information contact:

REALITY ENTERTAINMENT
POB 91
Foresthill, CA 95631

ph-530-367-5389 fx-530-367-3024

www.reality-entertainment.com

ISBN: 0-9777904-5-2

Printed in the United States of America

Contents

"The changing of bodies into light, and light into bodies, is very comfortable to the course of nature, which seems delighted with transmutations."
—*Sir Isaac Newton (1642-1727)*

Foreword

The story that you are about to read regarding our soul's "light body" anatomy and physiology activation process has implications for us all that are nothing less than earth-shaking revelations. For we are coming to see that our planet's purpose is to help us butterflies shed our cocoons made of dense-matter. To do this, we must restore our biosphere, our life-support system, to its optimal pristine, "green energy" light-matter configuration.

That is my mission, too, to restore the Garden of Eden. It was also that of paleontologist and theologian Pierre Teilhard de Chardin (1881-1955) who defined this eventuality last century as our emerging *noosphere*. "The noosphere is a 'planetary thinking network'—an interlinked system of consciousness and information, a global net of self-awareness, instantaneous feedback, and planetary communication. The task before us now, if we would not perish, is to build the Earth."

Moreover, when is the last time your family medical doctor—let alone a board-certified forensic psychiatrist—spoke to you about your *immortality*? Can you imagine what will happen to our worldview once this message that we do not die sinks into our psyche individually and collectively? It will electrify, self-empower, our global society to *go green* in ways that are truly unimaginable today. Let us pray our citizens get this message and implement corrective action to our biosphere before we become a breech birth. Indeed millions of us have our head stuck up our past both religiously and scientifically—and it hurts like hell!

John Jay Harper[1]
Executive Director
American Delphi Academy

---

1. Dr. Harper is a clinical hypnotherapist and author of *Tranceformers: Shamans of the 21st Century* at www.johnjayharper.com.

Chapter One
The Golden Man

I began meditating at age 12, shortly after one of my seventh grade teachers showed a film on transcendental meditation (TM). Much to the dismay of my Southern Baptist parents, I adopted the practice as a daily habit. For as long as I can remember, I felt a profound inner yearning to understand how the universe worked. My discussions with Pastor Simpson about the Holy Bible used to irritate him to no end.

By the time I was ten years old, I had read both the Old and New Testaments. My questions often centered upon my need to understand the violence and pain that filled the lives of the characters in the scriptures.

When I turned twelve, Pastor Simpson asked me to start teaching Sunday school to the younger children and the teenagers. One year later, I was asked to moderate the Sunday school discussions as the superintendent. During this time, I never let the church know that I had begun to completely embrace meditation practices as well as develop a spiritual philosophy that went way beyond what I was being taught then by Christianity.

My mother and siblings used to make fun of my meditative postures in fact. My brother, Dennis, even used to jump on the bunk bed while I meditated and throw pillows at me when he thought I was being too quiet. I made him pay for that many times over after he went to bed! You see I knew the sort of sounds that frightened him during the night, and I became quite adept at creating most of them at-will.

Within two years of starting the routine practice of meditating, I began experiencing emotions, visions, and thoughts that defied simple explanation. More so, while meditating, I felt more peaceful and whole than I did at any other time in my young life. As I grew older, my meditations changed. In my youth, the visions that I experienced were dreamlike and idyllic. After 25 years of TM and "Kundalini" meditations that raised my body's cellular rate of vibrations, my visions took on an intense and overwhelming tone. Sometimes I would emerge from my meditations completely enraptured. The scenes and images that I saw were beyond verbal description.

Yet up until my 37th birthday, I was an observer in my meditative world. However, The Golden Man changed that forever. I am not sure why he came to meet me, but the time that we spent together changed the course of my life.

The first time that I saw The Golden Man I was emerging from a long solar-meditation. During my residency to become a board-certified psychiatrist, I had adopted the habit of meditating while the Sun bathed my face. When I opened my eyes, I could clearly see a figure emerging from the Sun. At first I couldn't determine if the image was that of a man or a woman. But as the image coalesced, I saw that it was the rough outline of a man. He "stood" before me, floating. His physical features were faint, but I could tell he was smiling. He was roughly eight feet tall and surrounded by a softly luminescent golden light. He floated closer to me and in that life-changing moment I realized that I was witnessing my first transcendental, spiritual, vision. I didn't know if I should run and hide, or kneel.

The Golden Man smiled and asked: "What is your name?"

Somehow I felt that he already knew the answer to that question.

"My name is Mitchell," I softly replied.

I then mustered enough presence of mind to respond with a question of my own.

"What is your name?" I asked.

"My name is Djeuthi." His voice was resonant, like a soft echo. Louder than a whisper, but not quite up to normal conversational-tone level either. It was one of the most beautiful sounding names that I had ever heard: *Dee-jan-tee*.

"I have watched over you for some time now," he said.

"How do I know that I am not hallucinating all of this?" I asked, although I knew I was wide-awake. Furthermore, I could see him whether I opened or closed my eyes. I had learned over the years that visions, in their rarity, were clearly discernible whether my eyes were opened or closed. Simple mental images did not do that. Yet I still didn't know what he or it was exactly.

"If it is easier for you, then you may think of me as a figment of your imagination, though this approach will cause certain problems for you later," he stated.

"Problems? What problems?" I responded.

"You will soon realize that your imagination is not capable of generating the experiences that I will share with you."

"What experiences?" I inquired.

"Some might call them vision quests or, simply, 'shamanic journeys.' You might choose to call them teaching lessons," he counseled.

In that moment I realized that my life was about to change forever. He floated closer to me, touched me lightly on the forehead, and then vanished in a flash of light. I could still hear his voice resonating in my mind, even though I could not see him anymore. I realized that I had either had a spiritual breakthrough or the not-so-subtle beginnings of a mental breakdown.

Chapter Two
The Fateful Decision

For the next six months I avoided meditating. I debated with myself as to whether I had imagined the meeting with Djeuthi. I had gone through many years of rigorous meditation and training in an effort to raise my consciousness. There were times when I felt that I had attained wondrous levels of personal insight on a variety of topics. Inside however, I always felt that something was missing. I wanted to know about the inner workings of the soul. I wanted to meet God and ask him questions like why mom gave my little brother a name like ... Ronald? Well, maybe not!

But, seriously, I wanted to know for sure, without equivocation or doubt, the workings of the human soul—how it works and how it evolves? I wanted to know how that knowledge fit into a workable framework for spiritual growth and enlightenment? I wanted to have an honest-to-goodness transcendental spiritual experience!

Towards that goal, I had gone through hundreds of books, dozens of seminars, and literally countless hours of contemplation in an effort to learn more about my soul and how to evolve beyond my present level of awareness. Then, right before my eyes, stood the answer to my search. Yet as real as it seemed, I could not help but question the reality of my encounter. My training as a medical doctor had shaped within my consciousness a skeptical, doubting mind-set that defied my attempts at spiritual union with the cosmos-at-large. This alienating aspect of myself was intensely angered by the appearance of Djehuti[1] (See footnote at the end of this chapter for the origin of this most unusual name).

As I was to learn later, many of us have a filter; a "Doubting Thomas" aspect to our mind and that was the reason that it had taken me thirty years to open this doorway in the first place. In particular, I had to remove the "field of debris" called "history" from my mind's eye in order to see anew. The information that I've learned has convinced me that we are privy to only a small fraction of our spiritual birthright. The fruits of the spirit remain hidden by our ego—that aspect of mind that seeks separateness. So, over the next six months I examined my "close encounter" with Djeuthi in every conceivable manner.

First, I researched the most basic question: Is the human being a condensed Body of Light now? That is, do we "see as through a glass darkly" as Saint Paul put it biblically? Ancient texts do say that matter is only fallen spirit. Maybe we are light bulbs with the dimmer switch turned down low? Perhaps we are as a butterfly struggling to free itself from its caterpillar cocoon made of immortal light crystals?

Second, if so, has the existence of our "light body" been documented by historians and religious authorities already? To my utter amazement, I found a rather large database of literature on the subject dating back thousands of years at least. In fact, all the major spiritual traditions of the world demonstrated that enlightenment is not simply a one-time psychological event: It is a process!

Spiritual self-realization has progressive phases, or sub-stages, of transformation. That is, very real and tangible physical changes occur as a person ascends in consciousness through mystical or transpersonal experiences. In the last stage of enlightenment, according to esoteric teachings in various sacred traditions and schools, the cells within the human body are changed from matter, flesh, into pure energy, light. Through the so-called process of "transubstantiation" of the blood, skin, and bone, one actually transcends into a light being!

Activating Your Immortal Body of Light is the end goal of world religions.

In the Judeo-Christian tradition, this body is called the "resurrection body" or the "glorified body." Not surprisingly, Saint Paul named it the "celestial body" or the "spiritual body."

In Sufism, it is called "the most sacred body" and the "supra-celestial body."

In Taoism, it is called the "the diamond body," and those few humans who have attained it are called "the immortals."

In Tibetan Buddhism, it is called "the light body."

In Tantrism and various yoga systems it is called "the vajra body" and "the adamantine body."

In ancient Egypt, it was called "the luminous being."

Sri Aurobindo, a great Indian teacher and mystic, declared that the "divine body" is the ultimate goal of human evolution. He said dormant "seeds" of immortality exist within each of us now waiting to bloom and bear fruit. Thus, as the caterpillar carries within its DNA genetic memory bank—called a *genome*—the blueprint for the butterfly, we have an unimaginable transformation event ahead of us as well. For if I am correct, we, too, are to be "born again" as diaphanous, translucent, butterfly-like beings of light!

Indeed, only three percent of the three billion base pair genome of our DNA encodes for the construction of the physical body. Ninety-seven percent of these DNA base pairs appear to be totally inactive during the normal course of human life. So my question: Is it possible that the vast dormant potential represented by these billions of base pairs forms the basis for the formation of a higher state of physical expression for the body? Is it possible that the human body acts as a cocoon for a higher, more complex, longer-lived form which has the potential for immortality? Many scientists are exploring this hypothesis today.

Irish biochemist, Colm A. Kelleher, Ph.D. reports in "Retrotransposons as Engines of Human Bodily Transformation" that he wrote for the National Institute for Discovery Science: "The historical literature suggests that there are unusual physical, as well as psychological, consequences in humans to the attainment of the exalted state of mind known as enlightenment, nirvana, or samadhi. These reported changes include, but are not limited to, sudden reversal of aging, emergence of a light body and observed bodily ascension into the sky. This paper proposes a 'jumping DNA' or transposon-mediated mechanism to explain rapid and large-scale cellular changes associated with human bodily transformation."

In the process of my own research, I found a number of well-documented historical cases that seemed to bear out the reality of a multiplicity of a spiritual forms, including the light body, that are connected to the human body in everyday human experiences. One such incident was reported by an Italian writer named Ricardo Bandini in 1951 in his book Posito super virtutibus. He wrote that in the summer of 1930 while he was visiting Assisi on the last day of June, he witnessed the following remarkable event:

> At the Sacro Convento of Saint Francis I ran into a...Franciscan, a rather tall fellow with a beard, nice looking.... Seeing that he wore a beard I imagined he was a missionary, something I had desired but which problems with my eyes had made impossible. I asked him if he worked in the missions and he replied affirmatively and introduced himself as Father Maximilan Kolbe. He conversed with me about the Madonna ...Speaking...with great enthusiasm, he became, as I watched, transfigured, in a diaphanous form, almost transparent, and surrounded by a halo of light, all of which lasted

while he spoke...I found myself trembling with a sort of fear, filled with confusion—so moved that tears came to my eyes.

.   I can totally and completely sympathize with his emotions on this matter. He had witnessed a profoundly transcendental vision that was far beyond his ability to deny—or comprehend. Thank goodness, I found several more cases in the literature that helped ease my discomfort with Djehuti.

In 1899, Moslem and Christian Lebanese officials received reports of a great shining light that emanated from the grave where Maronite monk Charbel Makhlouf had been buried. The monk had died on December 24, 1898. The body had been buried in mud, not embalmed, and without the benefit of a coffin. Religious pilgrims even tried to steal pieces of his remains during this time. The phenomenon continued for 45 days, prompting officials to exhume the holy man.

His body was found floating in the mud, but was itself completely free from signs of deterioration, "as if it had been buried the same day." In 1950, Sister Maria Abdel Kamari was taken to the gravesite while suffering from a serious intestinal problem. She could not keep food down, had been bedridden for 14 years, and had already received the sacrament of extreme unction three times. While she prayed at the grave, she suddenly felt a powerful surge of energy and was able to stand unaided. Since that time, Sister Maria Abel Kamari has been completely free of her previous ailments.

On January 21, 1993, Nouhad El-Chami, a 59-year-old Lebanese woman, saw this same monk appear to her in a body made of light. She stated that she tried to see his face but couldn't, because the light coming from his body and eyes was too blinding and powerful. Pope Paul VI canonized this man as Saint Charbel Makhlouf on October 9, 1977. In another similar story, Clement Boccardi, secretary to The Venerable Vincent Morelli, archbishop of Otranto, wrote the following account of his employer, titled "The Servant of God."

While I was with the Servant of God during a visitation of the diocese of Castignano dei Greci'im house of the deceased Mr. Antonius Marini, I Iooked one morning into the Servant of God's bedroom, which contrary to his usual ways, he had not left yet. I observed the room illuminated with a radiance which to me appeared to be neither candle nor daylight—especially not candlelight owing to my observation in the course of the night that no candle had been lit because I slept in the adjoining room. The scene held a surprise for me, but I kept my counsel and reflected whether the light emanating from his person might not be supernatural in nature. Presently, I was approached by the master of the house, and told that he had looked through a keyhole of another door, and had observed the Servant of God on his knees surrounded by light. This convinced me that the illumination that I had seen in the room had not been due to the light of day or candlelight, nor some other natural source but to a supernatural action. The master of the house was a prudent man, highly esteemed for his moral rectitude, and possessed of a capacity for clear judgment.

In modern times, best-selling author and anthropologist Carlos Castenada declared upon the death of his spiritual teacher, shaman Don Juan Naguel, that he personally witnessed the old man's body transform into pure light. This ball of light then ascended into the air, where it was joined by a number of similar Light Forms that hovered above it. These beings then drifted away collectively toward the neighboring hills and disappeared through a spontaneous opening within the fabric of space-time itself. Clearly, there is much more physical "genetic" potential within us than our modern-day medical schools have heretofore suspected. So how do we activate these "jumping genes," so to speak? Perhaps, we don't need to *do* more, we need to "be" more often? In short, we must learn to "quiet the noise," the "chaotic chatter" within our minds and the "road rage" within our hearts.

There is a common theme running through all the major spiritual traditions of the world: *Be Still and Know God*. That is, these transformed humans had gone through years of meditation retreats prior to transformation—as a rule. There are always exceptions to everything. However, activation of the remaining 97% of the human genome—or at least the segments that we attribute to enlightenment—are stimulated by silence, the damping-down of the overtly critical-thinking cortex of the brain-mind complex.

My research has shown that our DNA is the Book of Life. It contains the secrets to life, death, and rebirth cycles within its cellular memory spirals. More so, I have witnessed firsthand that we are literally hard-wired to the cosmos through the infinite fields of electricity and magnetism that is consciousness in its polarized aspects. Speaking scientifically and spiritually, my encounter with Djehuti resulted in the opening of my third eye into the Fifth Dimension. Once I began to accept my interaction with Djehuti as "normal," I likewise resumed my meditations. "Normal?" Now there is a word I wouldn't have the luxury of ever using flippantly again.

1. There are two major root word origins of the name "Djehuti" or "Thoth":

Egyptian: Djehuti, Tehuti, Zehuti, Djhowtey
Greek: Thoth, Toth, Thot, Thout, Hermes Trismegistus

Although the names vary by culture and era, Djehuti or Thoth is the original god of wisdom. He is associated with teaching, fantasy, speaking, and inventions. He wore the head of an ibis-stork and carried writing tools, protected physicians, and knew of alchemy or high magic formulations. He was called "the Silent Being," no doubt a true paradox as his guardian role to spoken words. He was honored in the "Lord of Heavens" festival that was held on the Egyptian New Year Day (circa July 20th). See http://www.granta.demon.co.uk/arsm/jg/tris.html

Chapter Three
We Meet Again

Sometime after my initial meeting with Djehuti, I told my girlfriend Donna about the encounter. She attributed it to the number of hours that I put in at the hospital. She had a point: It was nothing for me to work up to eighty hours per week as a resident psychiatrist. Indeed, as Chief Resident, I had to cover the duties of a doctor who had taken sick leave then as well. However, even with the extra hours and the increased stress load, I had not experienced a recurrence of the "visitation" from The Golden Man—yet.

Of course, I knew that the major difference in my lifestyle before and after the experience was "only" the lack of meditation. I had stopped meditating, in fact, but I began to really miss communing with my inner self. I especially missed the subtle sense of expectancy that I got from "letting-go" of this outer reality and sinking deeper into the inner reality that is our soul. Ultimately, I surrendered to my intuitive "urge to merge" with the cosmos-at-large and decided to overhaul my entire daily routine in the process. For all practical purposes, I was preparing myself for a major expedition into the unknown and, therefore, I wanted to be in the best possible spiritual and physical condition.

Thus, I began to exercise five to six times per week. I changed my diet and stopped eating red meat in particular. Giving up my landlady's prime rib and mashed potatoes was no easy feat either. I also gave up pork. I stopped drinking the eight to twelve Sunkist Orange sodas a day that I dearly loved too. Finally, I made sure I got at least eight hours of sleep per night. I was ready, let the journey begin, or should I say, continue ...!

So late one Tuesday afternoon, after I had completed a long day of rounds and conferences, I settled into my familiar meditative posture near the bedroom window in my apartment. I had purchased a large meditation pillow and chair combination that I positioned near the trellis. The soft pillow cushioned my body and I wrapped myself in the purple silken robes that my mother had given me for Christmas. The Sun hung low over Philadelphia that evening, I recall, and the sky glowed with a deep azure-amber fiery color combination.

The setting was nearly perfect, although I could smell my next door neighbor's open-pit grill broiling mouth-watering steaks. Nonetheless, I turned my focus inward, ignoring those tantalizing smells that triggered longing memories of my last center-cut prime rib dinner with Miss Wayne. Why oh why did my landlady have to bathe that meat with that delicious red wine au-jus sauce? Well enough self-torture, I mused, I was committed to my meditation program after all.

As I allowed the Sun to bathe my forehead, I calmed my outer worldly thoughts. My mind settled into its familiar rhythms, and I could feel myself finding my center once again. Years ago, I had adapted a breathing technique that I now call the *Breath of Seven*. It has become my unique method for centering my consciousness.

It consists of taking one full, long inhalation, then emptying my lungs in two shorter, half-full exhalations. Then I breathe in two deep breaths and out four breaths. I continue this pattern in this way: three breaths in, six out, four in, eight out—until I reach a count of seven breaths. I then repeat the process at seven breaths in, fourteen out or, in other words, I repeat the process in reverse: Six breaths in, twelve out, five in, ten out, four in, eight out, all the way down to one. I repeat the entire process seven times. By the time I reach the fourth or fifth repetition in this cycle, I enter into meditative trance, a so-called altered state of consciousness.

Upon completing these breathing exercises this evening, I slowly began to feel an equal measure of fear and elation flow through my being, as I felt a presence enter into the room with me. My eyes were closed, but I could clearly see with my mind's eye the image of a large opalescent ball of light as it descended from the Sun into my bedroom. This particular vision persisted, however, whether I opened or closed my eyes in fact. Now I knew that he had waited patiently for me to return to my meditations all this time.

Within moments, I saw the form of a human figure outlined in the light. I could not see details of the face right away, but I could clearly see the overall dimensions of the image itself. He was almost as tall as the ten-foot ceiling in my bedroom. He floated gently within a glowing stream of brightly luminescent golden light—only slightly less brilliant than the late evening Sun. A few moments more and I could see his face and body structure. The figure was male but there were no external body appendages: hair, skin, nails, genitals, or anything. He was clothed in flesh that was fashioned out of pure light.

The image had some human facial structures: a mouth, nose, and eyes. And he radiated a strong aura of serenity, peace, and power. I summoned all my will power to make the image go away, but it persisted. Reluctantly, I resigned myself to the obvious: The being that stood before me was neither a figment of my imagination nor a hallucination that would subject itself to the lesser powers of my will. Whether I was ready or not, I stood face to face with an immortal man made of light.

"I have been looking forward to our next meeting, Mitchell." His voice resonated with the clarity of a clap of thunder and the discharged energy of lightning. His aura widened as he spoke, the iridescent colors shimmered blue and gold in the sunlight.

I was transfixed.

"I don't know what to say. For months I've wondered what I would say to you if we ever met again. And here, now, in the moment, I'm speechless."

Then he replied: "Perhaps words are not needed at this time. Take my hand and I will show you the why of my visit."

He held out his hand made of light-flesh. As his hand approached mine, it began to glow ever more brightly. If I wanted to see just how deep the rabbit hole goes, I was going to have to take his hand, and I had nothing to lose at this point. I stood up and grasped his slender fingers. As soon as I touched them, the bedroom disappeared and I felt myself hurtling through space toward a huge brightly-lit floating object.

Trying to get my bearings, I looked around and saw a blurry palette of stars and galaxies whizzing by me. I felt an immense jolt of electricity surge through my whole body. I was instantly invigorated and terrified at the same time. I had never experimented with drugs in college but I mused that this might be akin to a good trip on LSD. I also wondered if I was traveling in my spiritual body or my physical body.

"You travel in your true Form," he told me. "The physical body is but a shell for the habitation of your true self."

"You can hear my thoughts?" I relayed.

"And you mine. For the purposes of this journey, spoken words are unnecessary."

We slowed down as we approached a huge object that glowed brightly in the surrounding space. It was roughly spherical and ominously monstrous in its appearance. Shimmering violent pulses of red and orange light filled the void around us. The object was the biggest and most awe-inspiring thing that I had ever seen. It spun rapidly in many directions at the same time, and seemed to pulse with a wildly impossible force of life. It seemed to seethe with the energy of life itself. Gigantic tongues of energy and flame periodically shot straight out from its surface. The scene reminded me of images I had seen of activity near the surface of the Sun. This object, however, only faintly reminded me of a star. Somehow, it seemed alive, different.

"What are we looking at?" I asked.

"A human spirit." His thoughts washed over me like the soothing chords of a Chopin etude. I liked the effect that they were having on my senses.

"This thing is huge, or so it appears. It looks like it must be at least the ten times the size of the Sun. How can this possibly fit inside a human being?"

"It does not," he said. "The object that stands before you is a single human Spirit. Created within the Mind of God, it is a being of near infinite potential and power. Even though the Spirit appears to fill almost your entire field of view, we are approximately 400 million light years away from its core. Were we to venture much closer, your present form would not endure."

"How," I reflected, "is this Spirit connected to a person? I mean it is huge, monstrous even."

His reply was electrifying: "The Spirit never leaves the Mind of God. It is God's idea of the creation of a single human entity. As you can see, the potential that God places into even one person is tremendous. Only a tiny fraction of the Spirit is manifest in one individual."

"So all of this is one person's Spirit?" I mused again.

I had read something similar to what he was saying in a book on Gnostic philosophy. Now I was seeing the proof of their words for myself. Somebody else had obviously experienced the same vision.

"Yes. But, you must realize that each Spirit is a truly infinite being. Each Spirit influences the creation of an infinite number of souls in an infinite number of dimensions. Notice the flashes of energy surrounding the Spirit."

"Yes, I see them." How could I not?

He continued: "Each of these flashes represents the generation of a new soul fashioned from the essence of the Spirit. As they are created, they exist as only the tiniest essences of living awareness, clothed in raw divine creative energy. They have no individual awareness or consciousness as of yet. They still require further packaging and development."

"So you are saying," I tried to remain calm, "there exists one of these for each and every human being in the world?"

Nonetheless I was shocked at the implication. "Yes. Scientists in your world have a name for these objects—but little do they know that the objects that they are describing are the spirits of intelligent beings."

I knew that he was referring to quasars. I had read that there were large numbers of them filling the outer reaches of space, but no one knew what they really were or what function they played in the scheme of things. As far as scientists could determine, quasars were neither stars nor galaxies. However, they radiated more energy than either stars or galaxies. They were a complete scientific mystery.

For the next round of questions and answers, he and I simply went back and forth. I pitched a question to him and he tossed an answer back to me:

"How long has this Spirit been here?"

"Forever by your reckoning of time. It is actually older than the concept of time as you know it, as it was created before the conception of the space-time continuum in your universe. But that is not relevant to the purpose of our journey."

"How did we get here anyway?"

"Do you remember seeing bright lights and shimmering balls of energy sometimes during your visions?"

"Yes. I never knew what they were. I always thought that they were the result of residual light images from my brain."

"Your brain does not create your reality; it only interprets the information that it receives about creation. One of those shimmering balls of energy now spins before you."

"But I thought quasars existed only in outer space?" I was really starting to get confused now.

"Remember that what you see is not a quasar, as you might call it. It is a human Spirit. Also remember that everything you experience in the outer world exists in exact detail in the inner world."

"As above, so below?"

"Yes, that is correct. Nothing exists in the universe that fails to be represented in exact detail within your being or mine."

"So I traveled inside myself to see this spirit? Why?"

"It is your Spirit, Mitchell."

"My Spirit? How can that be? I mean look at that thing! It's huge—I mean, it looks HUGE!"

"All humans possess such a Spirit. Yours is no different."

"So for all these years I have been looking at my own Spirit and didn't know it?"

"Yes. You are now beginning to learn the correct understanding of your true origins."

This was getting to be fun! I was even growing accustomed to this back and forth dialogue style that we had established now. In a strange way, I was even growing accustomed to his presence. I began to wonder how long we had been traveling. My senses were starting to become disoriented. I needed a break although I wanted to know what manner of being this man Djehuti was now for sure, and where did he come from? I would ask him those questions but not before he returned me to my apartment.

"I want to go home," I said. "I need some time to digest this all this information."

"Very well. Pick out one of the sparks of light that emanate from the image before you."

"Why? Will that lead me back? I thought we would just go back the way we came."

For the first time, a tiny pang of fear surfaced from deep within my mind and barreled its way into my consciousness. I was totally dependent on this being that I barely knew to get me back home from God knows where?

He sensed my panic: "Do not be afraid. Follow the spark that you have chosen and you will be safe."

I calmed myself and focused my attention on one particularly intriguing spark of light that emanated from what was apparently my own spirit. It glowed more brightly than many of the other sparks around it, and appeared to be somewhat closer to my present position. I liked its vibrant blue and gold hues. I forced my consciousness to merge with the spark and followed it into the void. Instantly I was bathed in a sparkling flood of tiny rivulets of light. The sparks filled my being and washed over my mind like a flood. I could still see Djehuti, but his image was gradually becoming lost in a torrent of new images that almost ran together as they whizzed through my consciousness. I could scarcely believe what I was seeing.

When I focused my concentration on one of the images, I saw what appeared to be a large oak tree. It floated among the stream of images and blended once again into the background of light. Another image took on the appearance of a turtle—a giant sea turtle that stared back at me with ancient eyes and swam away amidst the tapestry of stars. Still another image appeared to be that of a single drop of water, glistening, yet still within the cacophony. Another image resembled an old woman carrying a large bale of straw upon her head. She grinned at me from some far away and distant world.

Three new images projected themselves prominently into my field of view. One seemed to be a large mountainous structure capped with snow and lined with pine trees and drying shrubs covered in ice. The second of the three images took on the appearance of an amoeba, undulating and writhing spasmodically in the river of light. The third image was that of my own body. It was sitting in my usual meditative posture near the trellis by my bedroom window. I willed myself to go closer to that image, and within an instant I was back within my body. I could at once feel the silk of my robe against my skin and the familiar softness of the down pillow that lay beneath my body. Djehuti floated silently above me: He was smiling.

"Am I back home?" I promised myself in that moment never to do drugs in my life. Ever, and I meant it. After this experience, there would be no need; you can't get any higher than outer space, can you?

"Yes. This is your home. You are safe."

Never had his statements sounded so reassuring to my ears. I wanted to kiss the floor of my bedroom and roll around on it in childish delight. I would have, too, but I had a ton of questions, and I desperately needed some serious time to digest the images that I had just seen. One question would not wait, however:

"Djehuti," I asked, "what were all of those images that I saw when I merged with that spark of light? For that matter, what was that spark of light?"

"They were images from your incarnations. Understanding that much, can you answer your second question for yourself?"

"Maybe but I don't know why I was so attracted to that particular spark of light, yet I recall that it did seem to have a much stronger magnetic pull to it than the others that I saw. When those images that you say were my incarnations were coming from my Spirit, I had sensed they were all connected to me somehow. So if by following it's rays back to my body, then that tiny spark of light has to be my soul?"

"Excellent! That is precisely what it is. Do you understand how it led you here?"

"Not exactly," I had to admit.

"The exercise that you just completed is the exact recreation of the journey that you take every night when you go to sleep. Your soul retracts back to the source of spirit, recharges itself from the vast energy stores in that space, then returns again to this body at the end of the night. In order to affect its return, safely, the soul must identify, know the correct body from which it originated."

"How did you know that I would pick the right one? There were a lot of souls out there for me to choose from. What if I had chosen the wrong one?"

"They were all yours in one incarnation or another, Mitchell."

Now that reply really *floored* me—all puns intended!

"Djehuti, what are you?" I was proud of myself for getting the question out finally.

"I am a man, Mitchell."

That answer was the last thing that I expected to hear from him.

"No disrespect intended, but in my opinion, it is a very curious man who floats in air."

"In my opinion, Mitchell, it is a very curious man who cannot fly."

With that statement, Djehuti began to fade from the room. His image gradually shrank in size and he slowly receded from my view. The luminescence that accompanied him disappeared, and when I opened my eyes fully, I was once again alone. I looked at my clock and I saw that only six minutes had passed since I had begun my meditation. As much as I didn't want to admit it to myself, he did have a point. At his level of physical and spiritual development, floating in the air and flying through the inner reaches of outer space was obviously normal. I was left to ponder the ultimate question based upon what I had just experienced. Perhaps, I had just in fact witnessed firsthand where our own evolution is taking us now?

Chapter Four
The Day My World Stood Still

I understood how Dorothy felt when she woke-up back in Kansas: There is truly no place like home after such life-altering experiences. I had just witnessed the most important event of my life and I felt very, very, different. The experience had changed me in subtle ways. For one thing, I was more at peace with myself and the world around me was bigger and more alive than ever before. I looked up at the setting Sun with a newborn's eyes to let the last of its softer rays stream into my pupils, as I felt the bliss that contentment brings with it sweep through me. Something had happened beyond my understanding then, and I had grown in ways immeasurable to modern scientific instruments, but there was no need to deny it now.

I slept like a baby that night.

And the next day I returned to work at the hospital with a renewed vigor and fire for life that surprised my colleagues—and me. I wondered how did I get so much energy from a dreamless night's sleep? I also noticed that something was different about my interaction with my patients, and for that matter, everyone else. Although I tried not to dwell on the experience that I had had the previous evening with Djehuti, as I still had to perform the demanding duties of my job, it was extremely difficult not to do so. My stream of thought sooner or later invoked those images of my previous incarnations, but as the day progressed I no longer had to struggle with them as much. After a while, they simply retreated inwards.

Nonetheless, I secretly wished I could share my experiences with someone. I wanted to shout and act like a soccer player who had just made the winning goal in the World Cup finals. But I couldn't. My residency program was conservative as you might well imagine. To make my situation more confining, the president of the American Psychiatric Association was also the Chairman of my Department of Psychiatry! Even though my academic and clinical standing was excellent, I dared not risk discussing my extracurricular spiritual activities with even my closest colleagues—let alone the boss.

Equally, at that time, I was the Chief Resident of the Department.

Psychiatry is the most buttoned-up, traditional of all the medical specialties. It is one of the toughest to get into for residency, too. In fact, only half of those who had started their internship with me now stood a chance to graduate four years later. Time, stress, pressure, and the rigors of long nights on call had thinned the field of potential survivors down considerably. There were other burdens for me to carry as well, as I wanted to be the first black male to ever successfully complete the program. I knew I could not afford to jeopardize my career period. Once again, as I had to do when I was a child, I was pretty much forced to keep my spiritual meditations to myself. In some ways, this situation reminded me of my Southern Baptist church days; I had to keep my mouth shut in order to survive socially.

Fortunately, I became very busy with meetings, new client admissions, dictations, and I also needed to see a nun who was dying of ovarian cancer. Her pain medication was not working sufficiently, and her doctors felt that depression was now complicating her condition. When I sat down with her I could see that the cancer had totally ravaged her body. She was a sixty year old, five-foot tall, seventy-pound skeleton. Her eyes were sad and clouded, but when she looked up at me as I introduced myself, she smiled. I took her hand and sat down to talk. She had only been a nun for five years.

In her life before the convent, she had been a devoted wife and mother. Her husband had died of lung cancer ten years ago and their only child had died in a car accident two years later. She had entered the convent in answer to a lifelong dream that she had never allowed herself to share with anyone. She had been diagnosed with ovarian cancer one year ago.

"I'm dying Doctor Gibson. I just want to go but they won't let me. Help me." Her plea came from the depths of her spirit. It almost brought me to tears.

In that moment a shaft of sunlight penetrated the drab sterility of her room and fell gently upon her face etched with wisdom born of pain. The light draped her body and outlined the areas that the tumor had destroyed. It then entered her eyes and disappeared behind her partially closed eyelids. I had never seen such a thing before. I tried not to let my surprise startle her.

"I will do everything that I can to help you, ma'am. How are you feeling today?"

"I can't think. I can't read. I can barely see. Worst of all, I can't pray. Can you imagine a nun who can't pray? I am such a sad thing."

Her voice was slightly more than a thin whisper. I had to crouch near her lips just to make out her words. A narrow stream of tears lined her cheek, and I took a tissue from her bedside. I wiped her face and threw the tissue in the basket near her bed. I knew that she was dying and her doctors had given her less than six weeks to live. If we could stabilize her pain medications and her depression, we could transfer her to hospice so that she could live out her last days in peace. How I wished that I could offer her more than antidepressants and kind words. But as I struggled to answer her plea, I noticed a familiar voice: Djehuti.

He asked me, "Might I make a suggestion, Mitchell?"

I could not see him anywhere but the sound of his voice was unmistakable. The moment was decidedly awkward and I wondered if my client had heard him as well. A quick glance downward toward her reclining form assured me that she had not.

"Fancy meeting you here. How did you do that? I'm not meditating now."

"There is a special connection between us now that could help you in your work. That is, if you are willing. This person is known to me, I can assist you in her care."

"How do you know her?" I challenged.

"I have seen to her medical needs in a number of lifetimes. Her condition is a recurrent one that has claimed her life on more than six occasions. It stems from her inability to reconcile her love of family with her love of the Creator. She feels an innate need to punish herself for desiring a family."

"What's your suggestion?"

I thought I might as well get what I could out of our interaction. My client seemed to have fallen asleep and that was reassuring. I wondered if Djehuti had been human in some past lifetime. How else could he have taken care of her medical needs?

"Ask her to forgive herself and release the tumor. There are entities around her who will then see to her further care. Following this, touch her on the forehead and awaken her."

I rebounded, "You want me to ask her this before she wakes up?"

"Yes. The request will be more effective if you speak directly to her Spirit while she slumbers. In doing this, you will help prevent her from repeating the cycle of manifesting this condition in her next incarnation."

I did as he asked. I then touched my client delicately on her forehead and woke her. Her eyes were bright and she smiled warmly. Even though only a few moments had passed, she seemed to be more at peace with her condition.

"I feel much better Doctor. Thank you. I think I can rest now, I will let you know when I get home."

Startled, I replied, "What do you mean?"

"You will see. Please, let me get some rest now."

I wasn't quite sure what she meant by her statement, but I respected her wishes and excused myself from the room. I went to the nurse's station and ordered a low dose of an antidepressant medication and something to help her sleep. I told them that I would return to check on her in the morning. I left the hospital to catch a few hours of sleep before my evening call shift. As I was driving home, I looked down and saw my beeper flashing. I then heard a voice that shook me. It was the lady that I had just seen.

"Thank you for coming by today Doctor. I am much better now. I understand what you meant. I won't do this to myself again."

And then there was silence. My beeper did not have a voice function. When I got home I called the Medical Unit and asked the staff about my client. The nurse on duty who had been assigned to her answered the phone.

"Did someone call you Doctor Gibson? How did you know?"

"Know what?" I puzzled.

"Your client just died a few minutes ago. She was a no-code."

"No, I didn't know. I was just calling to see how she was doing. Thank you, nurse, I will call Social Work and get them to notify her family."

After hanging up the phone, I sat there in the stunned silence for a few moments to recollect my composure. I didn't fully understand what had just happened, but I knew that something far beyond a simple break-through in meditation had taken place yesterday. I prayed for my client's soul, and lay down to take a nap.

I woke up two hours later and prepared for my evening meditation before driving back to the hospital. I placed my pillow near the trellis and slipped on my robe. I lit a white candle and placed it in the window and would let it burn all the way down to mark the passing of my client. I cre-ated this ritual for myself; it was my way of saying goodbye to them.

After I lit the candle, I closed my eyes to feel the rays of the after-noon sun brush my face again. I half expected Djehuti to appear, but he did not. I sat in quiet contemplation for more than an hour, slowly sifting through my new revelations.

I recalled, of course, that Djehuti had shown me my different in-carnations that evidently included all the rungs on the ladder of evolution. That means that God must create, for all practical purposes, an infinite number of souls that in turn incarnate within an infinite number of dimen-sions—and "bodies." Each of those souls begins life as a tiny spark of awareness in an atom, a molecule, a cell, ultimately a whole community of cells in the trillions that gradually, painfully make their way up to the human form.

I knew that the Hindus teach that soul-sparks transmigrate from one type of existence to another in complexity—for example, from an amoeba to a human being, but they also teach the principle of reincarna-tion. Incidentally, that is a belief that is shared by more than seventy-five percent of the world's inhabitants.

Today, I had seen a lady, who had been one of Djehuti's patients in another lifetime, release herself from her physical body and die peacefully. She then somehow manifested her voice over my beeper to thank me for helping in her time of crisis. Although her condition was apparently karmic in nature as Djehuti knew all about her illness. How did he know all these things? Who was he? I needed to talk to this floating man more often perhaps?

After our encounter today, I realized that I was no longer afraid of him. I pondered that he might have evolved from the human condition to that of a light being and maybe that has something to do with our own next step in evolution? Whatever the case, when I stirred from my meditation, I understood the events of this day much better and could return to work refreshed, contemplating that we, too, might have an immortal future?

Chapter Five
Unanswered Prayers

Once in a while, the universe graciously smiles upon you and life is a little brighter if only for a little while. My on-call shift that night was easy—mercifully. I had no new emergency room admissions, or calls from the wards. My girlfriend Donna and I in fact went out for dinner that evening at the Indian Delhi Palace.

I wanted so much to share my spiritual experiences with her. We had been dating for several months, but between my call schedule and her workload as a teacher and single mother, we barely had more than two nights each week together. I enjoyed her company. She took me out of myself and made me remember that I had a life, a real life beyond that of a professional caretaker. She could tell that something was different about me. I told her that I was working out more and taking better care of myself. That answer seemed to suffice for now.

Later that evening I went home and prepared myself to meditate before going to bed for the night. I sat down on my pillow and began the Breath of Seven. Tonight I felt centered, and thus my body settled into the rhythms that I associated with a deep meditative trance state easily. Before I could object, I sensed that my body was melting away. Indeed I looked down and saw that I was in fact rising into the air.

Calming myself now, I rose higher and higher until I could no longer see my bedroom. The sky opened above my head and I could see a thick bank of rumbling clouds rolling in toward the city. I rose progressively faster and faster until the earth below was no longer visible at all. Only the velvety black void of space lay beyond. In the distance I saw a dazzling white light that was rapidly speeding toward me. In a few moments, I was totally engulfed within it. The outline of a large human coalesced out of this brilliant cloud-like substance and spoke to me:

"Hello Mitchell."

Djehuti seemed so pleasant and serene. I wondered if he ever had a bad hair day. Humor helped me deal with the unnerving fact that I was experiencing an involuntary out-of-body experience.

"Hello Djehuti. How are you?" My casual reply seemed somehow strangely appropriate. Floating thousands of feet above the earth with a ten-foot tall glowing man does call for some seat-of-the-pants wittiness.

"I thought I would join you in a stroll," I retorted. "You seem to be so happy in your flight through space."

Djehuti resonated with my style: "A sense of humor? That makes me feel so much better. At least now I know that we have something in common other than our ravishing good looks!" He continued: "Humor is an important tool in coping with the complexity and paradoxes of creation; I believe it helps the soul in many, many ways. By the way, I'd like to show you something if you have a few minutes."

I agreed. "Sure, whatever you like. But you have to promise to answer some questions before you disappear again. You left abruptly last time."

"I apologize for my dramatic departure, but my presence was needed elsewhere. Take my hand and let's continue where we left off."

This time I knew what to expect when I grasped his fingers made of light. My body shivered slightly as his warmth and serenity flooded my being, and within seconds I felt at peace. My vision seemed to expand and grow, and I saw the world around me become suddenly aglow. The smell of ozone, akin to burning-oak filled my nostrils. We began to fly faster and faster. The stars whizzed by us in a near-blinding flash. Then we just stopped as suddenly as we had started seconds ago.

"Look down, Mitchell."

I turned my gaze to the space beneath us. As far as the eye could see lay what seemed to be billions and billions of large pulsating globular clusters. Cloud-like in their configuration, the clusters rose and fell with an almost lifelike rhythm. They seemed to parade to the beat of an unseen drummer. Tiny embers of golden light flittered among the images like moths swirling around some colossal evening fire.

"What are those things?" I wanted to know.

"Why don't you go find out?" he countered. "They are perfectly harmless."

I focused my consciousness on the clouds. Instantly I was drawn into the midst of them where swirling images melted into a mad cacophony of faces and scenes, as some of them grabbed my awareness. Instinctively, I forced my mind to bring into focus a clear image from the center of that maelstrom as a number of disparate scenes played themselves out before me.

I chose a relatively small dark-colored cloud and flew into it. Once inside, I saw the image of an elderly Oriental man with thinning dark hair, sighing as he bent over his bed. He seemed to be in pain, and the hurt in his eyes spoke of years of a life that had only been endured. Joy was not evident. The clock by his bed glowed in bright orange colors. The numbers flashed 4:30 in rhythm to some unheard melody. He watched the clock anxiously and mouthed some desperate words that I could not make out. In the corner by the bed I could see the glint of a thirty-caliber hunting rifle. He looked at me and turned away. He was crying. I couldn't see any of those firefly things around this image.

I entered another slightly larger and more brightly-lit cloud. A young girl appeared within its mist. She shrugged and half-smiled, awkwardly. Her hands looked as if she had been throwing clay, perhaps preparing a vase for the kiln that sat near her workbench. There were images of various sized plates and saucers scattered around her. Huge splotches of red, green, and yellow paint stained her smock. She was mumbling some words but I couldn't make them out either. They were only faintly audible and seemed to die away if I strained to hear them. There were a few firefly-like embers around her, but they too seemed to scatter and disappear after a few seconds.

Another, even larger cloud towered above all the others that surrounded it. It was filled with a wide palette of Jackson Pollock-like colors and images that danced and swayed majestically. This cloud was filled with millions of firefly-like images. Its very essence seemed to glow and pulsate. As I drew myself further into its midst, I saw the image of a small child kneeling at the side of a bed. The boy seemed to be no more than five years old. He was Oriental—maybe Japanese, as far as I could tell—and his eyes were piercing and brilliant. Unlike the other images, I could clearly hear his words. He was saying the Lord's Prayer.

I then looked to my right and heard Djehuti begin another series of questions and answers between him and me:

"So do you now know what these cloud-like objects are, Mitchell?"

"Yes. They are prayers. But why do some of them have those little firefly things and others do not?"

"Those flickering lights are the force of hope. When a human prayer is infused with intense hope, it manifests more quickly. As you can see, many of them, even the largest of them, have very little of this energy."

"There are so many of them. What happens to them? Where are the angels? Where's God? I always thought that when we prayed, God would hear us."

"You pose a very good series of questions Mitchell. Would you like for me to answer them verbally or would you like me to show you?"

This whole experience was starting to feel like being within a classroom preparing for an important examination with Djehuti serving as a Master Teacher. However, he never really told me the answers; rather he'd lead me to the place in the universe where I could "see" the answers.

"Show me," I responded. "You know me well, don't you, Djehuti?"

"In many ways. Do you see that spark of light at the uppermost region of the last prayer request that you entered?"

"Okay, I see it now."

Spinning far above the image of the child's prayer was a large yellow gem-like object. It reminded me of a beautiful marquis-cut sapphire with hundreds of perfectly cut facets on its face. Each facet gleamed with its own inner-light, growing steadily. As I forced my consciousness to focus intently upon this scene, I noticed the gemstone was siphoning all of the power away from the cloud-like prayer image, growing more and more intense in its brilliance. Eventually all of the essence of the colossal cloud-like structure was consumed by the yellow gemstone, glowing so brightly that I could barely look upon it. Understanding Djehuti's teaching style, I knew what I had to do: I flew straight into the center of the gemstone.

As far and wide as I could see, I saw a universe of experiences unlike anything I had ever seen before or even knew existed. Each of the facets of the stone had now taken on enormous proportions, as large as a small house structure. They shimmered in their own yellow and gold light energies. Above and surrounding these facets, I saw that a velvety blue mist permeated the interior of the stone, but I had no idea what its function was within this overall context. The facets had five individual sections and each section told a different story about its function.

I chose one facet and began to examine it. I could see row after row of arcane writing and one of the sections flashed brightly. The writing resembled Aramaic or, perhaps, Hebrew. As far as I could determine, the symbols were repeating one phrase or statement over and over and over again. I had no clue what it meant then. The letters were aflame as if white hot, glowing incandescently. When I drew closer to them I could hear a sound that reminded me of a cracking wood campfire or the softer, rolling boom of summer's distant thunder.

A second section displayed a series of choppy, discordant images, and no sooner had one image segment completed movement, another took its place in this dance within the center of the gemstone. The images displayed what appeared to be a collage of someone's lifetime events.

A third section generated tiny spheres of a bluish-green crystalline substance that disappeared almost as soon as it emerged into the surrounding atmosphere. When I drew closer and touched one, the object shattered into thousands of small shards. Each time one fractured, I heard a distinct but muffled exploding sound. One of the shards penetrated my arm and disappeared into it.

A fourth section seemed to be larger and more luminous than the rest. Small lightning-like protuberances leaped forward from its surface and died away into the vastness of the space surrounding the gemstone. This section emanated its own light. I saw a series of characters or letters within its central core, too, but the lightning interfered with my view of them.

The fifth and final section was by far the least luminous of all. It was misshapen and seemed to be loosely attached to the facet itself. I could clearly make out a word on its surface, and just as I was about to speak it aloud, Djehuti appeared abruptly by my side. He said:

"You are preparing to speak the spiritual Name of this person. To do so would bind you to his soul in ways that you may not desire later."

I hoped he wasn't going to play word games with me again, so I said:

"Before I even think of asking you what a spiritual name is, you have to tell me what I am looking at here. I am baffled."

Djehuti sensed my frustration: "Do you recall the young boy whose prayer towered above all the rest that you saw earlier?"

"Yes, the Oriental child" I shot back.

"Mitchell, when you followed that spark of light from his prayer into the gemstone it led you to this center place, the very inner sanctum of that young boy's soul."

"His soul?" I asked. "The energy of the prayer went back into his soul?"

"In a manner of speaking, but the process is considerably more complicated. Let me explain to you the form of this place," Djehuti offered, "and then what happened to his prayer will become clearer to you."

Chapter Six
The Living Soul

For the first time, I was happy that Djehuti had chosen to simply talk to me about the gemstone and spare me the theatrics. The fact that I now floated within a human soul was mind-boggling enough to contemplate for the moment. Yes, no doubt, I looked forward to hearing how all of this fit together now.

"Mitchell," he began, "the human soul is shaped very much like a diamond in the rough. It is the central unit of life within the human body. Each soul weighs about three-quarters to one and one-half grams, depending on its level of evolution and maturity. The more mature the soul, the heavier it becomes. The facets that you saw are indeed components of the soul's structure. There are 617 facets within each soul. Each facet is comprised of five individual sections. You examined them in the following order: the Word, the Actus, the Prima, the Nomen, and the Spiritual Name. I want you to consider the function of each of these sections in turn."

"The first facet that you saw, the one that seemed to contain arcane symbols, contains a Word of Power. A Word is a creation of great power. Do not think of this Word in the same way that you would an ordinary combination of letters. This Word is capable of affecting reality on a direct level. When properly invoked, a Word will create an elemental change in the form and structure of reality. Some Words heal the body, others force it to grow. Still other Words invoke the power necessary for the implementation of specific body, mind, and soul functions. Some Words create chaos and death."

"Each facet contains a different Word and therefore each individual soul has at its disposal 617 Words of Power. The power to invoke and carry out the dictates of a Word is produced by the Spiritual Mind. The Spiritual Mind is an immortal function of the Spirit, the deepest level of cosmic consciousness, and as such it creates and guides the intelligent functions of the Soul."

"The Soul, in turn, creates the limiting, mortal or human aspects of our subconscious mind, which is concerned with maintaining the biological rhythms of the body, such as our heart rate, breath, immune system functions. Can you imagine what would happen if you had to consciously "think" to breathe, or regulate the cells in your body to fight off infections? However, the Spiritual Mind invokes Words that are transmitted via the soul to the body. Once there, the Power of the Word will carry out the delicate emotional, mental, and physical readjustments, the literal re-balancing of the body—if not otherwise interfered with by negative thinking or catastrophic illness. There are many other functions of the Word that we will discuss at a later date."

Of course, I had read of Words of Power in my study of spiritual teachings. This is a major theme in the mystical writings of St. John too: "In the beginning was the Word, and the Word was with God, and the Word was God" (John 1:1, KJV). Every culture one turns to from the Hebrew, Egyptian, Greek, or Mayan, the ability to "speak the Word" and communicate with the gods is a cherished gift of wisdom. It does not take a genius to understand why that is true.

In particular, I remember the story about a shaman who had invoked a Word of Power to create a rainstorm. The tribal elders of a village consulted him during a severe drought. For there had been no rain in the area for seven months and the crops of the region were in dire need of moisture. This wise man entered the village, stood calmly in its center, looked up into the sky and uttered a single unintelligible Word.

Within moments the sky darkened and the ground became covered with a soaking gentle rain for the next three days. As the rains continued, the waters of the neighboring river began to rise. After five days, the entire region surrounding the village began to flood. The elders called the shaman back and begged him to stop the rains! Once again, he spoke a single unintelligible Word as he looked upward into the rain clouds. The torrential rain showers stopped upon command just as they had started.

According to Djehuti, all humans were blessed with the gift of these Words at the beginning of creation but were lost in the cyclic earth changes that occur as we go from Golden to Dark to Golden Ages—again and again and again forever. The Hindu priests call these cycles of consciousness-to-unconsciousness, the "yugas," while others call them the Age of Information to the Stone Age. No matter the terms, I thoroughly enjoyed listening to Djehuti speak further on these topics. Many things that had confused me were being put into place, finally.

He continued the discourse:

"The second section," Mitchell, "that you examined was the Actus. It contains all of the information regarding the past, present, and future lifetime events of an individual that in truth are parallel lives; that is, happening all-at-once. Since the cosmos is a hologram—a whole message—at the highest level of consciousness, ultimate reality is experienced simultaneously. The human beings that are awakening into cosmic consciousness now have the ability to read the information contained within this section of the facet. You would call them gifted, or 'psychic.' But this skill is contained within everyone. It is simply the case that it has not been activated—yet. Every event, thought, action, word, and deed that an individual will ever perform is recorded on the Actus section of each soul."

"The third section that you examined was the Prima. It is the substance from which the body, mind, and soul repair their organic structure. In its most basic form, the Prima is nearly inexhaustible. It may be shaped into any element or material that is required by the universe. For example, when the body is injured and needs to repair cells in an organ system or skin tissue, a Word is invoked by the Spiritual Mind, that reactivates the Prima to perform the task required. All structures, whether they be dense physical matter or light matter, are made of Prima material. That is how this substance penetrated into your arm and merged with you: Everything that was/is/will be created is formed via Prima. Those streaming particles that you intercepted were on their way to create some "thing" for that soul. You might say you got caught in the middle of an information exchange."

"The fourth section that you inspected is called the Nomen. It is the Name of God that is written upon each facet of the soul. Each soul has only one Name written upon it, and this Name is repeated on each facet like a hologram. The Nomen embodies the properties of God that each soul is created to embody as it matures. The average soul lives for twenty-five to thirty-five thousand years, though it may live much longer depending on its ability to gather regenerative life forces into itself, and the extent to which it develops the ability to use these Words of Power consciously."

"The final section that you examined contains the Spiritual Name of the individual soul. At the time of its creation, each soul is given a unique name. This name is your true name and does not change from lifetime to lifetime. When the Creator interfaces with an individual, he uses this name. When the true Spiritual Name of an individual is spoken aloud by another, those two beings are bound to a cycle of birth and rebirth together for a period of no less than seven lifetimes. That is why I stopped you from speaking the name of that soul earlier."

"As I have presented this discourse to you, Mitchell, you are now aware of the science of soul facts that have only been shared with certain small groups throughout history up until today. However, I believe that you have adequately prepared yourself for the reception of these truths through your medical schooling."

Now I had lost track of time, and space, so mesmerizing were the words of instruction that I had just received then. Djehuti's teachings on the soul were unlike anything I had ever heard or read about previously. In fact, I didn't know such an in-depth analysis on the structure and function of each aspect of the soul was even possible. I didn't know that it was so complex either. What happened to the simplistic story that I was taught in Sunday school, such as you need only live a good life here, die, and go to heaven there? I mean, Djehuti was implying that we are like children today that are being asked to grow-up and assume responsibility for our actions within the cosmos at large.

He was right; I needed some down time, so to speak!

I touched Djehuti's hand and within an instant I was back in my room. I looked at the clock and over an hour had passed. Outside, a gentle storm had begun to sprinkle rain over the city. Djehuti was nowhere to be seen, but I silently thanked him for our time together anyway. I wearily dragged myself up from my meditation pillow and made my way into a refreshing shower and then after a quick snack, I lay down—within minutes I fell fast asleep but awoke within a crazy lucid dream.

The Word of God Comes Alive within a Dream

A big man in a light gray suit lumbered into the brightly-lit diner and sat down lazily at the counter. No one seemed to notice him at first, but the waitress, who was much too thin to be pretty, looked at him wearily. She had been counting the minutes until she finished her shift.

"You're looking quite lovely tonight, my love. A fine sight for these tired old eyes." The big man smiled broadly at the young girl.

"You know, I get off work in fifteen minutes. I hope by that time you would have kept your tired old eyes and lines to yourself and ordered something so I can go home."

"In that case, Miss, I'll have a shot of Jack Daniel's for myself and a bowl of bananas and a Perrier for my friend here."

"What friend? You came in here by yourself."

"I have to admit, he is sometimes easy to miss. Pardon my manners; I should introduce myself and my friend. My name is Mr. Ibis. You may call my friend Vegas Bill."

The man pointed to the large brown and orange baboon that sat at his side. The waitress was sure that the baboon had not been there a few moments ago. She was sure that an adult baboon could not have entered the restaurant without her noticing. The baboon grinned at her and scratched his nose with its long dirty nails. In the booth next to the odd couple, a tall thin man sat quietly and tried to avoid the melee. The waitress did not seem to notice him.

"We don't serve monkeys here, Sir. You will have to leave and take him with you."

The waitress was angry, but she wanted to avoid escalating the situation beyond her shift. She really wanted to slap the guy and shoot the monkey with the thirty-eight revolver that the owner kept in the drawer by the cash register. The baboon stood up and pulled a deck of playing cards from mid-air. He passed a long and loud pocket of gas out as he sat-up and howled to himself.

"Good one! Now, Miss, would you be so kind as to pick a card from my deck."

"Monkeys can't talk. Why do you have a deck of playing cards? Get out of my diner!" She realized that she might lose this battle if she let it go much further.

"Good lady, I can assure you that if you don't pick a card, he will do much more to your lovely establishment than, shall we say, spice up the place."

Mr. Ibis slapped the baboon on the shoulder and, grinning, stood by his side.

"Oh, alright. I'll play your stupid game." The waitress pulled a card from the baboon's deck and held it in her hand.

"Now what do you want me to do with this?"

"Don't show me the card. Keep it hidden. Now, if I guess which card you're holding, will you give me some peanut butter to go with my bananas?" The baboon stared at her with bright piercing eyes that reminded her of her Uncle Clayton's French poodle. The tall slim man watched on, but said nothing.

"This is so stupid. Okay, go ahead and guess."

"Very well then.   I think you're holding a full house, aces-high, with a pair of deuces in the boot."

The girl wondered how a baboon could learn to play cards. She also wondered why it would guess that she had a full house when she remembered clearly pulling only one card. She wished the owner was there to kill the monkey so she could go home.

"Look here. I'm calling the police if you two don't get out of here now!"

Mr. Ibis walked over to the cash register and touched it lightly. It promptly turned into a large stack of slightly used Gideon Bibles. Mr. Ibis then strolled over to the baboon, took him by the hand, and began to dance a lively jig. The baboon joined in and, without breaking their merry rhythm, they skipped giddily out of the diner onto the street. The waitress watched them continue their unlikely promenade as they disappeared down the rain-dampened highway. A huge watery full moon illuminated the buildings near the diner with a bright silvery light that was almost bright enough to read by. The waitress closed the door behind the unlikely pair, locked it, and sat down by the front of the counter to read a verse from one of the slightly used Gideon Bibles. Exploring the Word of God seemed significant to her, even more so than getting off-work at that moment.

Chapter Seven
Life is But a Dream Sweetheart

The dream seemed to last for hours. I had no idea where such an unlikely combination of characters could have come from either. The whole scenario was hilarious: A talking baboon playing cards and a strange man dancing under the moonlight almost seemed like some drug-induced fantasy. I had been writing down all of my dreams for almost a year.

For the most part, they didn't make much sense, but once in a while one of them seemed to catch my mind's eye open. This one seemed particularly meaningful. I had purchased a book on dream inter-pretation a few months ago from a bookstore on South Street. A baboon, a man in a gray suit, a waitress, a diner, and a full moon didn't seem to add up to anything of significance according to the Dream Compendium. But I filed the images away in my notebook anyway, got up, and pre-pared myself for the coming day. Djehuti's words from last night still rang clearly in my head: "... you are now aware of the science of soul facts that have only been shared with certain small groups throughout history up until today."

Throughout the day my mind kept going back to the hilarious image of Mr. Ibis skipping down the road, arm-in-arm with Vegas Bill. Every time I thought about it, I chuckled to myself. Later that evening, Donna and I went into town and visited one of our favorite bookstores in the Ardmore district. I loved to sift through the dusty old tomes in search of that one pearl that someone had been given or thrown away. My own home library on spirituality and metaphysics had grown to over one hun-dred volumes. Still, I felt that I had much to learn.

"Hey Mitch, look at this one." Donna didn't fully share my enthusi-asm in this area, but she was supportive. She had found an encyclopedia on gods from different cultures around the world.

"Now this does look interesting," I said as I flipped through the pages and spotted some familiar deities that I had studied in college and high school. The section on Egyptian Mythology definitely caught my eye. I glanced at the names, and one in particular stopped me cold in my tracks. Next to the inclusion on the god Thoth, I saw a name that I had only seen in my meditations: Djehuti. After I regained my compo-sure, I sat down on the brown leather ottoman that lined the wall near the bookcase. I stared at the name for a full five minutes I guess. I was shocked and totally speechless.

"What's wrong, Mitch?" Donna was understandably surprised by my reaction. I debated as to whether I should talk about my discovery with her—or not. Yet she would find out sooner or later if we were to get our relationship to last long-term I realized.

"Remember the being that I told you about that I met in my meditation?"

"I do, but we decided that he was just a figment of your imagination. Probably a result of you doing three on-call nights at the hospital in one week."

"I don't think so anymore. I think he might be real. Look here." I showed her the inclusion about Thoth. The name *Djehuti* sat next to Thoth's name in **bold black letters**.

"Remember what I told you his name was?" I queried.

"Yes, *Dee-gan-teee* ... or something like that."

"Look here, there it is. Right next to this deity named Thoth."

"Are you trying to say that this thing you saw is a god? Mitch, that is absurd!"

I saw that this conversation was not going to go as hoped. I decided to drop the issue altogether. I did not even bother to show her the associations about the moon, the ibis, and the baboon that were also detailed extensively next to the name.

"Maybe you're right, Donna. I had never heard of that name before he appeared in my meditation. It is not a very common name. Have you ever heard of the name Djehuti being associated with Thoth?"

"No, but that doesn't mean anything. It could all just be a coincidence. If you want the book go ahead and buy it so we can go and get something to eat," she snapped.

Donna was beautiful, intelligent, and a lot of fun to be around. However, in that moment, I decided that our relationship would always have certain uncomfortable limitations. I guess I had known that for some time now, but this moment had made the point abundantly clear.

"Okay, we can go," I surrendered without a fight.

The rest of the evening passed uneventfully. I dropped Donna off at her apartment and told her that I had to get some sleep before my next on-call shift. I really wanted to go home and look up everything I had in my library on Thoth, and I knew that she didn't wanted to join me in that discovery research process—or at least not yet.

That night, I read everything that I had on my bookshelves about the "gods" of Egypt. Djehuti was the name that was most commonly referred to in my search of the literature. The name Thoth, in fact, was a later title given to him by the Greek translators. The implications were simply staggering. For if true, the being that I had been meditating with was none other than one of the most famous of all of the Egyptian deities himself.

Djehuti (a.k.a., Thoth) was a very busy god too. He supposedly taught mankind the alphabets used in language construction as well as writing, astrology, mathematics, medicine, and architecture. He also showed the Egyptians how to build the pyramids it was claimed. There was even a legend that connected him to the creation of the world via something called The Sacred Words of Power. I sat stunned as I reflected how he just taught me about those Words and how they were part of every human soul's make-up. I, of course, truly wanted to know why he had chosen me as a contact out of 6 billion-plus people on this planet. And I also wanted to know why he sent me that strange symbolic dream—if he did.

But, nonetheless, everything was slowly starting to make sense now.

Djehuti's sacred animals were the ibis (Mr. Ibis), and the baboon (Vegas Bill). The moon was sacred to him, and legend states that he had introduced playing cards and games to humanity. The healing arts, dream interpretation, and spirituality also fell under his expertise. Djehuti was likewise credited with being *the* expert in the hidden knowledge of the human soul.

So how did I make contact with him—or he me?

This much I discovered from my readings: A religious group called the Gnostics—literally those who *know* the truth—believed that mankind possessed the innate ability to contact the gods directly for themselves.

They were at one time a very large and powerful movement, too, but with the advent of the Christian church in Rome about 325.A.D. their ranks shrank. Indeed, they were brutally murdered to stamp out this wisdom according to recently recovered *Dead Sea Scrolls*. For *direct conscious contact* with *God* is the major founding tenet of the world's great religions, if we accept the experiences of Abraham, Moses, Jesus, Mohammed, and Buddha as valid.

More so, if these stories are not true but rather imaginary figments from the minds of delusional visionary men, then there would be no *bibles*, no churches, no temples, no synagogues nor any reason for their existence either. Worst, if we felt that these were all liars, then the very bedrock of our society would crumble into chaos as we in fact see happening, as mankind follows no clear-cut moral code of conduct anymore—other than the rules made by capitalism. For the most part, modern man has assumed that "speaking" experiences with God are superstitious nonsense, not to be given credence, thus our "gods" are self-made billionaires.

We look at creation through the eyes of scientists, politicians, businessmen, athletes, journalists, singers, and even writers. They are our *Harry Potter* priests that seek to bewitch us. University research facilities, sports arenas, movie theaters, shopping malls, concert halls, and luxury resort complexes have become our new places of worship. Research studies, television newscasts, magazine articles, newspapers, and Wall Street spin-doctors have dampened down our ability to think for ourselves. The illuminating "numinous" experience has been consigned to holy men and philosophers—an age long ago—no longer a legitimate goal to seek for oneself in contemporary society. At least, many "fundamentalists" would have us believe that is the case, but that is not what the Greeks taught in their temples. These priests chanted:

"Know Thyself"

(This is the translation of the original admonition "*Gnothi se auton*" inscribed on the Sun god Apollo's Oracle of Delphi temple in ancient Greece.)

Thus, after I had read everything that I could find on Djehuti, I became curious about the number of people who had experiences that paralleled my own in our modern world. According to a recent survey of 20,654 people conducted by author and paranormal researcher Brad Steiger, a large percentage of folks believe wholeheartedly that they have experienced the supernatural. A couple quick samples of the data reveal that thirty-seven percent believe that they had seen the form of an entity they can identify only as a Light Being, while thirty-eight percent believe that they have witnessed the physical presence of an angel.

If one assigns those numbers to the population at large percentage wise, millions of Americans believe that something otherworldly exists more than the dogma preached to them by the science and religion puppeteers combined. In numbers that defy simple explanations, Americans are not letting their strings be pulled by authorities, experiencing reality in a manner that more closely parallels that attributed to the mythology of the gods. I was not alone in my supernatural close encounter after all. Maybe we ought to conduct a worldwide survey to determine what is preventing all the others of our species from "seeing the dead" come alive?

For instance, in a survey of 321 people, British psychologist Susan Blackmore reported that 12% of her study group reported out of body experiences (OBEs). Most occurred when resting, but not asleep, and lasted one to five minutes on average. The respondents reported these OBEs variously as lucid dreams, flying dreams, hallucinations, body image distortions, psychic and/or mystical events. Gertrude Schmeidler, a researcher and emeritus professor at the City College of New York, reported that 12 surveys showed "Yes" answers between 4% and 98% of the time when people were asked whether or not they ever had an out-of-body experience. It really matters how you ask these types of questions in the surveys evidently. Again, no matter the "size of the sample" or percentage, just seeing those numbers was comforting.

Beyond a reasonable doubt, every day people around the world are experiencing the supernatural realms and the supernatural beings that inhabit them. To deny the existence of a higher reality is to deny the possibility of something greater than our mind and the human ego does not handle this possibility very well. We tend to rationalize and explain away that which does not vanish upon request. In truth, our close encounters with the cosmos at large is getting stronger and more active today than it has been for eons as documented by Richard Heinberg in *Memories and Visions of Paradise: Exploring the Universal Myth of a Lost Golden Age*. "Whereas human beings once lived forever, could fly, and could visit Heaven at will, they have now become earthbound creatures who are, in Eliade's phrase, 'limited by temporality, suffering, and death.'"

Be that as it may, the entities that we call gods from mythology seem to have an undeniable way of hanging around me. I now faced that reality on a far more personal level. Djehuti still represented a supreme mystery to me although I sensed a purpose in his visits. I also sensed an underlying connection between us that belied the differences in our physical appearances. There was something in his voice, a knowing that bothered me. I wanted to know why he was in my life. Why not Osiris, Ra, Isis, or some other deity? Why Thoth?

Well I sighed; you don't get these answers I am seeking from books and surveys alone: so I prepared for my long overdue evening meditation. It was late and I knew that if I didn't start now, I would soon be fast asleep.

I pulled out my robe and sat down on the pillow near the trellis by the window. The full moon hung high in the Philadelphia sky. I gazed at it for a few moments before I closed my eyes. I saw it smile at me! The full moon smiled at me, twice!! I blinked hard and looked again. But the moon maintained its toothy grin and began to change form. It began to swirl and pulsate with an almost ominous hoary luminosity. It fashioned itself into a human being. Within moments, the form filled the whole window before me. I recognized the outline immediately.

"Nice entrance!" I had to give Djehuti points for style.

"I am happy that you enjoyed my display. I am sure that you have questions for me. I see that you have made certain 'associations.'"

"I most certainly have. Are you the Egyptian God known as Thoth?" Part of me almost didn't want him to answer. A deeper part of me knew the answer already.

"I have not heard that name in a long time."

"Is that your name?"

"Yes, Mitchell, it is. I have many names."

"You are a God?"

"I am seen as such in some cultures. I do not wish you to see me in that way. My relationship with you and with many others in humanity is much more intricate than the word God would allow."

He admitted it. I didn't know if I should celebrate or kneel. I decided to let wisdom prevail and just listen to him.

"Please tell me why you have come to visit with me.   Why me?"

"I commune with many humans in this way. You are not the only one, Mitchell. However, my visitations with you have taken a decidedly more personal format. Your persistence in meditation has opened certain pathways in your being that permit greater latitude of contact between us."

"When I saw your name in that encyclopedia I almost dropped to the floor. I couldn't believe it. I had only read about Egyptian Gods up until now."

"Mitchell, I am not Egyptian. Let me explain some things to you so that this connection will make more sense."

"Albert Einstein correctly stated that matter and energy are interchangeable. Humans incorrectly assume that all beings are composed of physical matter. Just for a moment, imagine that when a human child is born to its mother in your world of physical matter, another equal and opposite child is born in another world. This second world is composed of a different form of matter. Let us call that form of matter; light-matter. Both children would grow and mature in the safety and security of their own worlds without ever knowing about each other. But, they are connected in that they are the same being."

"At the moment of creation, all matter and energy existed in the same place and time. When reality sprang forth from its place of birth, energy and matter separated to some extent. However, they did remain linked in many ways. In truth, light-matter and physical matter were created at the same time and continue to coexist."

"At the moment of creation, the awareness and intelligence of all sentient being existed at the same place and time. When life sprang forth from the point of creation, this awareness and intellect spread itself over a vast field of possible realities. These realities, however, remained connected by their central point of origin and their association with light-matter and physical matter. All forms of physical matter are connected to an equal and opposite form of light-matter."

"Energy equals intelligence and awareness. Consequently, the more energy a form has at its disposal, the more intelligence it is likely to possess. For centuries, humans have witnessed the existence of their light-matter counterparts. You have called them angels, gods, demons, and every manner of supernatural term that you could fathom. I am not a god, Mitchell, though I am often worshipped as such."

"So, you and your race are made of light-matter?" I sheepishly re-joined.

"Yes."

"And you are connected to humans who are made from physical matter?"

"Yes, though you are only partly made of physical matter. Re-member you are connected to the light-matter part of yourself through the moment of creation. All humans are related in this manner. There is a deeper level to the connection that you must understand."

"Tell me," I begged.

"You are part of a continuum of consciousness that is unbroken even unto the Mind of the Creator. The light-matter part of you is not just one being, but rather an unbroken series of beings who become suc-cessively more intelligent and more complex as they ascend the scale of Cosmic Consciousness. Your ancestors worshipped these beings as gods when they interfaced with the physical counterpart of themselves. I do not desire this manner of relationship with you."

"You may view reality as being divided into multiple-levels of Cos-mic Consciousness. This supreme MIND of GOD has the ability to create physical matter out of light-matter by simply "speaking" it into existence. This level of your being creates your stream of thought, initiates your dream patterns, and guides your karmic development. It supervises the overall development and evolution of the physical form as it experiences successive incarnations too."

"Mitchell, I am here to reveal that you have successfully contacted your fifth-dimensional Higher Self. This level of consciousness is the inter-face to all the multiple dimensions of reality, the gateway to God."

"You are me?" I stammered.

"That is correct."

"How did I manage to contact you?" I demanded.

"In many ways, meditation is similar to diving into the ocean. Sometimes you make a shallow dive, other times you dive deep. During one of the latter times, Mitchell, you visited my realm. I followed you back into this world and watched you before I made my presence known."

"So let me get this right. My consciousness exists on a number of dimensional levels that I know nothing about. At one of those levels, I exist as a being called Djehuti or Thoth? Is this why the person we call Jesus Christ stated that he was in God and God was in him and when you saw him you saw God also?"

"That is correct."

"And you are a god?"

"I have been worshipped as such, but I prefer to have a different relationship with you. Remember, I am connected to many humans, not only you."

The world seemed to get a little smaller. I needed to take time to think and figure out the world that was being given to me by this being.

"Let me think for a while. I need some time."

"So be it. We will meet again soon, Mitchell."

Djehuti then began to shrink in size. His form glowed with a faint glimmer of silver and disappeared into nothing. The room was dark again. I was alone. I removed my robe and put it away in the closet. I climbed into bed exhausted and fell fast asleep.

Satin Sheet Dream

The distinguished-looking older man moved closer to the young girl as they lay quietly. He loved the smell of Royal Satin sheets. He loved the feel of 600-thread count cotton. It was a fetish of sorts. He ran his fingers through her dark blond hair. He had always loved the almond smell of her long curly locks. She stirred to his touch and roused her-

self from her slumber. She knew that he was much older and that they had only recently met at the diner. When he ran out of the place with that monkey, she thought that she would never see him again. He had been so nice to her. She realized suddenly that someone was playing with her right but tock. She also realized that she felt the unmistakable feel of fur on her lower calf. In that moment she looked up from her pillow and saw the large baboon that she had seen earlier that night. Standing silently in the far corner stood the tall thin man from the bar. She wondered why she warranted all this special attention.

Thank you for the fried chicken and the coochie, Ms. Donna." Vegas Bill grinned as he ran his fat callused fingers along the girl's leg.

"I didn't give you any coochie you filthy monkey."

"That is strictly a matter of opinion, Miss. You see, my companion enjoys the more, how shall I say...'visual' aspects of our encounters with the female persuasion." The man sprang to the baboon's defense and placed his hands gently on the girl's shoulders.

"Any voyeuristic tendencies that I have developed during the course of our relationship are strictly intentional." Vegas Bill had risen from the bed and helped himself to the girl's black leather bra and teddy set that lay by the bed. He pranced around the room while he displayed his new treasures like a drunken supermodel.

"Why do the two of you have to act like this? You are crazy! Absolutely insane! Both of you get out. I don't know why I let you talk me into this in the first place." The girl jumped out of bed and ran into bathroom.

"He was right about one thing, Miss. The chicken was deeelicious." The man grinned slyly and lifted himself from the bed. He took the baboon by the hand and joined him in the modeling session. He had helped himself to the girl's robe that lay on the floor. Together they broke into a rousing rendition of the Marvin Gaye song "Let's Get It On." "I'm reallllly tryyyyying baaaaaby!" The tall thin man watched the proceedings silently, shook his head, turned to his right, and walked straight through the closet door.

Chapter Eight
A Hard Day's Night

This dream woke me up laughing at the insanity of the entire scenario once again. I guessed that perhaps now Djehuti was laughing with me as well. I wanted to ask him why he was sending me a serial dream that made no sense—or did it?

I looked at the digital clock near my bed. The red numbers and letters glared at me in the darkened room: **3:33 a.m**. Oh well, I sighed, I had a lot to think about and sleep was the farthest thing from my mind anyway. So I began to ponder the events of the previous day to see if I could connect-the-dots.

Clearly, during my meditations, I slipped into a level of consciousness called the fifth dimension, or I should say, I shifted my mind's eye into that realm at least. But what did Djehuti mean by his statement: "I am your fifth-dimensional form"?

Of course, I realized from studying science in college that the fifth dimension is considered the origin of light itself. Physicist Michio Kaku revealed in his book *Hyperspace*, "This alternative theory gave the simplest explanation of light; that it was really a vibration of the fifth dimension, or what used to be called the fourth dimension by the mystics. If light could travel through a vacuum, it was because the vacuum itself was vibrating, because the 'vacuum' really existed in four dimensions of space and one of time." One of the themes that kept resurfacing was how are we human beings and God connected to the source of light? In ancient times Thoth (a.k.a., Djehuti) had been worshipped as a being of light—as are all "savior gods" within every culture throughout our world.

I recalled that Albert Einstein had discovered that matter was a condensed, "trapped" form of so-called "standing wave" light energy. His ideas that were in part responsible for the creation of the atom bomb indeed came to him as a vision within a meditation as a young boy. He imagined himself traveling into outer space on a light beam. This "thought experiment" became the foundation to his basic and revised "theories of relativity" in 1905 and 1915, respectively. This "theory" was proven to be an undeniable fact and our planet has never been the same since this trapped light within a couple pieces of radioactive rock was unleashed to destroy two major cities in Japan to end WWII. So if matter and energy are but two versions of the same substance—light—then it is possible that all life forms co-exist as light energy and solid matter. Djehuti had certainly confirmed to my satisfaction that this is the truth now.

Moreover, mythology is replete with stories of light beings of great power performing miracles that range from creating physical objects out of thin air to healing the sick from their low vibration condition. It seems that merely being in the presence of light beings is desirable for that reason: It self-empowers us. Every culture has stories of contact with beings of light. According to Djehuti, these divine light beings are but an aspect of Our Higher Self that can expand and contract multi-dimensionally throughout space within an infinite field-of-mind. It as if we are simply caught within a web of dense threads of matter-energy now. But how could light beings co-exist in the past, present, and future simultaneously? Equally, is it the case that we don't really travel through space at all, rather that time is what life is made of? In this regard, I loved the comment by poet Jorge Luis Borges: "Time is the substance from which I am made. Time is a river that carries me along, but I am the river; it is a tiger that devours me, but I am the tiger; it is a fire that consumes me, but I am the fire."

Einstein himself stated: "People like us who believe in physics, know that the distinction between past, present, and future is only a stubbornly persistent illusion." He postulated that time travel is one of the effects of relativity since as matter moves faster; the force of time slows down around it. There are particles of matter called *tachyons* that travel faster than the speed of light and are capable of traveling backwards in time, at least theoretically. I suppose a higher level life form composed of a sufficient quantity of energy could conceivably move back and forth in time at will. I had seen Djehuti's powers to transform, so I mused that he probably moves through time-space as easily as I drive my car around town following a specific highway matrix.

We, too, move around in time and space, albeit much more slowly. For instance, if I were to fly from New York to Los Angeles in a supersonic jet that was also vibrating at the speed-of-light, I could technically arrive before I left. Time-travel is possible, in other words. Given enough energy, matter does travel back and forth in time, thus I could understand how light beings could exist in the past and the future, but how was my consciousness and Djehuti's consciousness one-in-the-same? How was he connected to so many humans?

That question led me back to the concept that all life is energy in various states of condensation. Djehuti said that he and I were beings connected to a continuum of consciousness where even the gods were "descended" from other gods and so on and so forth ad infinitum throughout the cosmos. The implication is that humans were likewise descended from the "body" of the gods. Could this "body" be Cosmic Consciousness itself? As I pondered this connection, I began to see the truth. Millions of people regularly report contact with highly evolved beings in UFOs, just as many people continue to report contact with divine beings in OBEs. Could these supernatural events be related? That is, is there a similarity between aliens and angels, too?

Of course, these paranormal reports are dismissed as fanciful hallucinations for the most part. I, too, had discharged them, primarily because my thinking had been programmed to label such things as illogical. What if these higher energy aspects of our own selves were using these "visits" in an attempt to educate their own denser aspects? It would be just like the human race to throw away such a golden opportunity to evolve, wouldn't it? Our warlike nature is really a dead-end in so many ways but especially when we fight in the Name of God.

Ironically, all of our major religions are based on contact with higher beings from other dimensions. I could see now that I was making the same mistake in perception that my ancestors had made. I understood why Djehuti wanted a different relationship with me. He was probably just as curious about me as I was about him. In a way, his study of me was no different than my study of my own inner anatomy and physiology in medical school. The red blood cells, inner organs, body chemistry, and nervous system of my body represented a dimension of reality that is as foreign to me as I would be to Djehuti. From his perspective, when I wandered into his realm unexpectedly, his reaction was no different than mine would be had my own red blood cells formed a smiley face as I looked at them under a microscope! I vowed then that I would investigate this "phenomenon" just as he did—with courage, open mindedness, and a sense of humor.

I wanted to learn as much as I could from our contact given that it might end at any moment. In that sense, we are at the mercy of Our Higher Self. I knew several things to be true however. For one, all humans were part of a continuum of consciousness that extended right up to the Creator himself. Second, some of these aspects of ourselves are vastly more intelligent than others. In our arrogance, we have wrongly concluded that we are the last word in the lifecycle progression of evolution. We might be at the top of the food chain on this planet but what about other solar systems? Seemingly, we are embryos waiting to be born into the cosmos at large. Suddenly, I felt like a caveman who just stumbled onto a 747 Jumbo Jet parked in the forest.

Moreover, I desperately wanted to share my new revelations. Donna and I had planned to drive down to Baltimore to visit the Inner Harbor and see the new aquarium. We needed to talk and unwind from our pressure-cooker lives. I wondered how I would break the news of my revelations to her and if she would accept them—or not. As fate would have it, after I showered, dressed, and was walking out the front door to leave for work, the phone rang.

"Hi Mitch, it's me, Donna." I was totally shocked. She never called me this early in the morning unless something was going on.

"Good morning. Is everything okay? How are the kids?"

"Oh, everything is fine with the kids. It's you and me that I'm worried about. I just want us to be normal. Like everybody else, you know. You are into some weird things. I worry about you. I don't think you should do this meditating 'thing' anymore. You are changing and I don't think I like it."

She had no idea how right she was. I was changing and for the better. At this time in my life I was pretty damn far from being normal too. Meditation was an integral part of my life. I intended to go deeper; much deeper than I had up to this point. Some of the people in my life would never understand or accept the process that I was going through and I was the one that had to accept that not them.

"I am on my way to work; can I call you later today when I finish rounds?"

"You always have something else to do. I want to finish this now! Not later, when it is convenient for you. Now, Mitchell! I want you to stop this stuff you're doing and come to church with me on Sunday. I want you to focus on our future and let this research or whatever it is you're doing go away. I want you back."

There is never a good time for an argument. I wish I could let her know just what I was really thinking and feeling. The true expression of my revelations and my passion would be lost in the moment. I cared about her and the kids, but before things got completely out-of-hand, I needed to address the situation.

"Donna, I realize that you have some concerns about my work and my research. I want you to respect what I'm doing and share it with me. There is so much for us to talk about. Donna, it is really wonderful. Let me show you. So many things are opening up inside of me."

"That's just my point. You don't know what these things are. You might be letting your work affect you more than you realize. I think you should be careful. Listen to me Mitchell, do this for me. Do it for us."

She pulled the "us" card. I felt insulted and misunderstood at the same time. I guess I knew that this moment was coming. I was already late for rounds and this discussion was not going to end smoothly. I did my best to keep my cool.

"I can see that you are concerned. I have never felt better in my life. My work and my research have enhanced my life. I don't think that you can fully appreciate that. I don't like the insinuation that I have somehow become adversely affected by what I am doing. You just don't know me that well if that's what you really think. I respect your religious and spiritual beliefs. I am asking that you respect mine now."

"I respect the fact that you are passionate about what you are doing. I'm concerned that you're looking into areas that are best left alone. Come to church with me. Let's pray about this. I'm sure you will see that I'm right and that you should let this stuff go. It scares me."

"Simply going to church is not going to change my passion Donna. I am sorry you're scared. There's nothing to be afraid of. I have to be who I am."

I realized that this was going nowhere good. I knew what I had to do. If she felt this way now, she would never accept my need to go further with the work.

"Donna, I'm sorry you feel this way. I think we would be better off not seeing each other for a while."

"So you're saying you would rather break up than go to church with me and let this weird research go?"

"Yes. I can't give up who I am to cater to the needs of another person, especially someone who doesn't understand me. I couldn't live with myself if I did that."

"And I can't live with you if you don't."

At that moment, she must have slammed the phone down. I heard a loud click and then silence.

I thought I knew her better than that. She seemed so angry. I had never heard her sound that controlling. In a way, I suppose she was reflecting back to me all my remaining fears and insecurities about the journey I was taking. Donna had been a mirror for the person that I used to be. That person was deathly afraid of change. He was also afraid to follow the beat of his own drummer and listen to his heart speak to him. I suppose I had become quite the people-pleaser. She knew that about me, and she played that card beautifully.

I bit the bullet and tried to call her back, but there was no answer. I left a message at her home and left for work.

I tried to call Donna every hour on the hour throughout the day. I knew that the relationship was over, but I wanted to talk and make more sense of the situation. I didn't want our friendship to end like this. And to make it worse, later that day, around 3:00 p.m., one of the interns went home with the flu. My attending supervisor asked me to cover for the night. This intern had unfortunately been scheduled to be on-call. I had little sleep the night before and the argument with Donna this morning had really made a mess of my day's energy reserves. This added burden didn't help at all.

Today was going to be a hard day's night.

As Chief Resident, the responsibility fell on me to either cover the night myself or find someone who would. I called all the residents and interns who were eligible for call that month. Of course, none of them were available. I had to do it myself. This day was shaping up to be a wonderful sampling of random inconveniences.

Thankfully, the rest of the day passed uneventfully. I even had a chance to sneak home and get a change of clothes for the night. Sometimes, a night on call could be a really good night's sleep and nothing else in fact. We all cherished those times of course. Sometimes, the gates of Hell opened up and every demon that ever beset mankind made it his business to lead some poor soul to the psychiatric wing of the Emergency Room. That night was to be one of those nights I came to see.

The first call came at 6:30 p.m. The orthopedic resident on call had admitted a woman who had broken her leg during a fall. She claimed that the Devil had made her jump off her second floor banister onto the street below. After her leg was set, I admitted her into the Psychiatric Acute Care Unit (PACU). We called it simply the "Pack." This unit held the most disturbed clients in the entire hospital. When I began the night, the census in the unit was two. The unit's maximum capacity was ten. By night's end, I would fill the place and then some.

As the night wore on, I could hear Donna's concerns ring more loudly in my head. Even though I was very clear as to my direction with meditation, I continued to wonder just how much the illnesses that I worked with on a daily basis would impact my journey. This night would answer that question once and for all.

The next call came at 8:15 p.m. I had just finished tucking my first admission into the Pack when I got another call from the ER. The surgical resident had just admitted a patient who had been injured in a car accident. Apparently the man, a 54-year-old Vietnamese cook, had been using the street drug "speed" and tried to drive home under the influence. He ran off the road and hit a small truck parked on the curb. Luckily, his injuries were minor. He became paranoid and began to see white elephants peering through the windows. I could hear his screams in the elevator two floors away. He didn't like elephants evidently. I gave him a strong sedative and admitted him to the Pack.

I had noticed with the first lady that I admitted that there was a fuzzy, almost misty, layer of filmy gauze-like material around her body. I initially attributed this perception to my lack of sleep the night before plus the argument with Donna, if not the stress of the shift alone thus far. Indeed I was quite overdue for a fatigue-induced illusion or two. But there was something remarkably different about what I was seeing. As though there were intention, purpose to the energy I saw around these clients.

The next call I got came at 9:20 p.m. A young boy had tried to hang himself in his next door neighbor's garage and the paramedics brought him in for evaluation. Fortunately, he was not successful, but he still needed to be seen by a psychiatrist. Tonight, that would be me. I walked into the examination room where the boy was waiting and I immediately noticed it. Surrounding him was a thick inky black film that seemed to hover over his form. The boy, a young black teenager who couldn't have been more than 13 or 14, sat complacently in the corner. He didn't look up or move in any way when I entered the room. He wore a red and white sweatshirt with faded denim pants. His feet were bare. I could plainly see the rope burns across his neck from the abortive suicide attempt. His eyes were the color of dark lumps of cold asphalt. He said nothing to me when I attempted to talk to him about the earlier events of the day.

Just as I was about to leave and write up the admission orders for the Pack, I saw a familiar glow materialize in the corner of the room. Djehuti's form glided over to be by my side. I could not help but wonder facetiously if I could get him to take my beeper for the rest of the night and cover my shift.

"I would be happy to cover for you, Mitchell, if you thought your colleagues would accept my presence." I had almost forgotten that he could hear my thoughts.

"You know I was just kidding, right?"

"We haven't much time Mitchell. You are aware of the disturbance hovering over the clients that you admitted this evening?"

"Yes, I wondered what that was. What is that stuff?"

Djehuti beamed: "I would like to show you something. For the moment however, you must warn the nursing staff of this child's impending emotional collapse. Observe."

At that moment, the dark inky film surrounding the boy changed color and flared into a bright reddish-orange hue. He seemed to be surrounded by a corona of leaping flame. I wondered how I could see this phenomena but something inside told me to leave immediately. Within moments of my closing the door I heard a loud crash in the room. The crash was followed by a series of yells and smaller banging noises. The nursing staff called for Security and within seconds the boy was subdued. Three Security guards and two male nurses were needed to hold the child while a sixth nurse administered the sedative cocktail that I had ordered. Djehuti had warned me of the child's explosion. When the unit had calmed down, I sat down to write the admission orders for the Pack and dictate the report for the evening's events. Just then, I saw Djehuti appear again.

"I am happy that the child did not harm you, Mitchell. His eruption was eminent. Do you recall the coronal discharge that you witnessed prior to his explosion?"

"I remember. You were telling me about what that was before I left the room. And by the way, thanks."

"You are welcome. I would not see you harmed in any way. The discharge you witnessed is related to the development of your sixth sense sight. Due in part to the time you have spent in my presence, your mind's eye is opening into the Fifth Dimension. You will begin to see reality on a different level now. It is my hope that I will be able to guide you in the use of this faculty. The substance that surrounded the boy, for instance, is part of a level of reality that is associated with emotional and mental disturbances that emanate from the soul. This child has been suicidal for several lifetimes. Unfortunately, he has successfully completed the act in at least three separate incarnations. The substance that surrounds him and the others you have seen is a condition of the soul that indicates extreme fragmentation."

"What is fragmentation?" I asked, eagerly wanting to know more.

"During the process of healing itself the soul will sometimes lose some of its 617 facets. This is the case in severe emotional trauma such as rape, suicidal ideation, life-threatening injury, or circumstances in which the person's integrity of thought is compromised as in combat. Under these periods of extreme duress, the soul will attempt to discharge the excessive negative energy buildup that results from the experience by throwing off the memory contents contained within these facets. These facets are then lost to the individual until the soul repairs itself either in this lifetime or another one."

"On the emotional level of creation, the filmy material that you saw serves the same purpose as blood on the physical level. It carries life-sustaining information as sensations. When an individual suffers a serious blunt trauma to the body, this is often accompanied by an issuance of blood. The same occurs on the emotional level during severe emotional trauma. The darker the film, the deeper, longer standing the trauma and the more sensory input is deadened, or lost, temporarily. The brighter the film, the more acute the associated trauma and, hence, a better opportunity for immediate interventions. Hence, the coronal flare that you saw around the boy that preceded his eruption."

"So the soul breaks down and bleeds off its energy akin to blood in the body?"

"As above, so below. In truth, the body's functions follow those of the soul very closely. There will be a number of patients tonight that will allow you to witness a wide variety of emotional phenomena at this level of creation. I will guide you in the proper understanding of these energies."

With that statement, he disappeared and left me to contemplate if my clients had seen Djehuti as clearly as I had? Oh well, I was happy that Djehuti was teaching me what the energies meant and at least that question had been answered. My journey with Djehuti was becoming a very beneficial if not routine experience now. In fact, it may have just saved me from certain injury at the hands of that child. There was even a possibility that I was going to become a better physician as a result of our interaction. I had always wanted to understand the phenomenon of Spiritual Sight better too. I was not foreign to this potential as I had experiences when I was in medical school and as a child that indicated that an inner as well as outer vision co-exists. But I had no idea just then how much of an integral role it would play in my future work with clients. When I finished the intake dictation and the admission orders, I left the ER and made my way toward the deli for what I could salvage for supper. On the way I called Donna's number again: No answer.

Meals—as well as sleep—can be a luxury for residents on call. Yet I managed to get two of Mrs. Denson's famous chilidogs before she closed the deli for the evening. This was no time to go "vegetarian!" I'll do that on my time. Albeit before I could sit down and enjoy the respite, my beeper went off again: 10:45pm. This night was still early. The number for the Geriatric Psychiatric Unit vibrated alive on my waist. Beside the numbers for the floor flashed three red sixes. I shot up from the table, grabbed my snack and made a mad dash for the elevator. Three red sixes meant someone had died on the floor.

I really didn't like seeing the three sixes given my religious background as a child. When I first started internship I couldn't believe that reality could play such a cruel joke: Six-Six-Six. But there they were and they always meant something bad was going down with a client as well. When I arrived on the floor, I found the nursing staff moving in a flurry of tightly choreographed activity. The nurse in charge of the floor summarized the situation as we quickly prepared to apply the proper code procedure.

Mrs. Lane was an eighty-seven-year-old lady who suffered from severe recurrent depression.   During better times, she had been a music teacher in the northeast part of town. She had three children and over seventeen grandchildren. I had admitted her to the hospital on at least three occasions during the last eight months. Seeing her lying there in a pool of blood draped in a morass of tubes, plastic lines, and electronic wires saddened my spirit. She had often told me that she wished she could just die. Life, she said, "was not meant to be lived like this." Her body was no more than five feet tall and she weighed a mere ninety pounds. She had not responded to medication and her physicians were contemplating the possibility of shock therapy.

As we worked on her I could not help but notice a clear blue mist rising from the chest area of her still form. It coalesced into a roughly spherical ball shape and then hovered in the corner of the room near the door. A few moments later another similar misty blue sphere emerged from her lower pelvic area and joined the first ball near the door. I tried to ignore the figures, but just as I turned back to her body to administer a shot of medication to stimulate her heart, a third clear blue structure emerged from her head. It was slightly brighter than the previous two forms and somewhat smaller. It joined its predecessors near the door. I watched in shock as they merged within seconds. As they converged, a ghostly phantom of Mrs. Lane appeared. She glanced at me with her kind blue eyes and smiled. I wondered if the staff could see her. I looked around the room and realized that everyone else was totally oblivious to her presence in the corner.

I had been awake for more than thirty long, hard hours. Hallucinations were definitely the order of the day at this point. Yet I wondered what other illusory goodies were in store for me tonight. Just then Djehuti appeared beside her glowing form. I could feel his mind reaching out to mine to communicate but I silently projected to him a plea to wait until I had finished with this emergency, please. He moved gently to my side and touched my shoulder whereupon I heard his voice in my mind.

"Mitchell, you are observing the departure of this one from her physical body. The three orbs that you saw earlier were the projected essences of her soul preparing itself for her transition."

If he was referring to Mrs. Lane's death, I was a little shocked. Even though she was quite elderly, I was sure that we could bring her back.

"Can you help me bring her back? I want to save her life." I figured that I had nothing to lose by asking him.

He counseled me: "When the soul coalesces in such a manner, each of the three components that you witnessed join together to form the afterlife astral body of the departed. This vessel, in truth, is the same figure that takes its place in the growing fetus at conception. In turn, they represent the physical, emotional, and mental aspects of the growing entity. There is a fourth aspect to this grouping, guiding the spiritual aspects of the human being's growth that does not enter into physical incarnation. During the sleep phase, certain unconscious states induced by trauma or trance, this fourth aspect of the soul coordinates the out-of-the-body activities. You have witnessed this soul's passing, Mitchell. Your administrations will at best support the tiny portion of life force energy that remains with the cells at the departure of the soul's components. Mrs. Lane, as you have known her, has already departed. Observe."

I looked toward the door at Mrs. Lane's soul form. It began to glow brighter and shrink smaller at the same time. I saw her smile again at me, and she managed a tiny wave with her right hand. In a few moments, the form had totally disappeared.

Mrs. Lane's body got colder as we furiously continued our code. Djehuti stood alone in the corner by the door and watched silently as I coordinated my efforts with the Medical Resident and Intern who had joined the resuscitation efforts.

After forty minutes, we managed to return only a feeble pulse to the body that lasted for a couple of minutes and then faded out again. Other than the oxygen, medication, and vigorous CPR that we were providing, Mrs. Lane no longer had a living, self-sustaining physical body. I looked at my watch and noted the time: 12:02 a.m. I tapped the Medical Resident on the shoulder and shook my head. She nodded her head in agreement. The entire team knew what had to be done, so in unison nurses, doctors, and attendant support staff stopped what they were doing. We looked at each other in silence. One of the nurses was crying as I took her hand and walked us out of the room together.

Time of death was dutifully recorded.

Death was a constant companion in our business. Sometimes it came from suicide. Sometimes accidents were the cause. At other times it came naturally. Yet no matter the method, to the medical team, death oftentimes meant losing a stranger that you had grown to know, respect, and care about very deeply.

Kathy Haynes had been a nurse on the Geriatric floor for two weeks and she had taken care of Mrs. Lane on the night shift nearly that entire time. She had graduated from nursing school only three weeks ago. I welcomed her tears, as my observation is that level of humanity by older caretakers is sadly missing. This job can harden you—if you let it.

"She was such a nice lady, Dr. Gibson. I liked her." Kathy placed her head on my shoulder and we sat by the main computer in the Nurse's Station. I didn't know what to say, but I felt that some words were necessary.

"Kathy, I have a feeling she's in a better place. I think life goes on elsewhere. I just can't believe that God would give us one life and nothing else."

"I feel the same way. Do you believe in reincarnation, Dr. Gibson?"

"As a matter of fact, I do. Otherwise, Kathy, the gathering of life and death experience makes no sense at all. I think that even before we die, some force inside of us prepares us for the next life. I think Mrs. Lane knew it was the right time. I think she let go and is at peace now."

Kathy was very intelligent and I was enjoying our conversation despite my somber mood. She appeared to be maybe 5 years younger than me and had beautiful honey-colored skin. Her eyes flashed with a sparkling light that danced when she moved her head. I wished that I could tell her about my real insights and convictions about reincarnation. Nut my thoughts quickly returned to Donna and the massive amounts of paperwork that faced me after tonight's shift. My beeper went off and the only too familiar digits of the Emergency Room erupted into view.

"Maybe we can talk later, Kathy. Are you okay?"

"Yea, I'll be all right. Thanks for taking a minute to talk with me, Dr. Gibson." She rose slowly from her chair and gave me a long hug. She walked back toward Mrs. Lane's room and prepared herself for the ordeal of dressing the body for transfer to the morgue.

I looked at the beeper again and steeled myself for the next emergency that I was to face. For a brief second, I let myself ponder Djehuti's insights. How did he know that Mrs. Lane would not return to her body? Did the appearance of the three orbs always mean imminent death? Would my second sight ever become that developed? These answers would have to wait.

I had a patient waiting upon me that had attempted suicide I was informed by Charge Nurse Grace Johnson, who had been in the Emergency Medicine Department for over 22 years. Prior to nursing school she had owned an antique automotive business specializing in Austin Healy convertibles. She ran the ER with the same degree of British spit and polish that had made her a legend in the convertible marketplace.

At 5'2", 265 pounds, she was a force of nature, but at 2:41 a.m. in this stressful setting, her stature became surreal. Indeed you just don't see people like her during the daytime; they all seem to prefer the night shift. She had never married and her main passion in life at this time was raising pedigreed Russian Blue kittens.

"Good morning, Dr. Gibson. Ready to go to work, sir?" Her clipped English tongue was particularly snippy at this hour. The only voice I wanted to hear was the one telling me how cute my mouth was when I snored, I wisecracked to myself.

"What do we have on the agenda, Miss Johnson?

"Well Doctor, for your evaluating and examining pleasure we have Mr. Boris Lanauzuky. He is 83 years young, loves horses, and tonight he took a stroll from North Germantown down to Center City in his boxers."

"That's at least 15 miles, and its damn cold outside."

"He doesn't seem to mind. He hasn't stopped walking since he arrived at hospital. A cute chap, he is, Doctor. But wait, that's not all. We also have Miss Adeline French, a 17-year-old beautiful young lady who fell into a silent stupor earlier today during calculus class and has refused to speak a word since. And by my own calculation that's 11 hours and 30 minutes give or take. Her family is waiting at the desk to see you."

I could see that Miss Johnson was enjoying the misery that she was heaping upon me. But I felt sorry for the poor souls who found their way into the ER tonight. They were not going to get their money's worth from a doctor who had only had two hours sleep in the last 48 hours.

"Do we have anyone else waiting to see me?"

"Oh my yes, I almost forgot. The police brought over a gentleman from City Hall. They say they found him sleeping by the entrance to the Court House downtown."

"What's so unusual about that? Have them take him to County."

"Well you see Doctor, he was naked, drunk, and he had no ID. He told them he was an "elf" and that's your specialty, isn't it?"

"Did he say why he thought he was an elf?"

"No he didn't. But you should know that he likes to sing old Elton John songs. That's all for now Doctor. Enjoy." Miss Johnson curtsied, twirled around like an aging barrel-chested ballerina, and marched down the hallway humming the lyrics to "Don't Go Breaking My Heart."

Why didn't I choose dermatology or something that had no duty in the middle of the night? Three new evaluations to perform, two of those not communicating, and an elderly man who probably forgot to take his bipolar medication. Sometimes, though, the really "crazy" cases that you see in the middle of the night had a way of waking you up. At times like these I, more often than not, enjoyed the insanity of it all. Tonight, I needed the stimulation to keep me going. I started with the elderly gentleman first.

Mr. Lanauzuky didn't know where he was or why he was sitting in his red silken boxers. He was an elderly white gentleman who was no more than five feet four inches tall and he might have weighed 90 pounds soaking wet. His skin was wrinkled with an odd sort of bronze-like tan. I wondered if he had been a sailor. He was draped in a hospital blanket and paced the room like a caged panther looking for an exit. He looked at me with a sly half-smile and shouted "Take the A Train." That was enough delusional behavior: I started to leave the room and write up his admission "ticket" order when Djehuti appeared.

"Busy night?" He floated serenely near the doorway. Mr. Lanauzuky looked in his direction and smiled.

"Hey buddy, who said you could float in my room?" Mr. Lanauzuky could see Djehuti. This was the first time that someone besides me had seen him as far as I could verify.

"He can see you! He can see you!" I was excited. Mr. Lanauzuky was not going to tell anyone anything for a long time. Manic psychosis would preclude recollection of these episodes. So I was not afraid to talk in front of him.

"Yes he can. I hope this brings to an end your own fears of impending insanity." Djehuti did not seem surprised that Mr. Lanauzuky could see him.

"I suppose another visual confirmation, even a psychotic one, does lend a larger degree of reality to your presence. Not that I doubt you at this point."

"Hey guy, let the Doctor do his work! Go get your own shrink!" Mr. Lanauzuky was determined to preserve the sanctity of our doctor-patient relationship. He seemed to be angry. Curiosity got the best of me; I had to know exactly what he was seeing.

"Mr. Lanauzuky, who are you talking to?"

"The same guy you're talking to, Doc. That big glowing guy that's trying to barge in on my dime." Mr. Lanauzuky then launched into another chord of "Take the A Train."

"Sir, tell me what this guy looks like to you."

"He's tall … kinda funny lookin' … bald-headed … he ain't got no skin or nothing … matter of fact…he kinda looks like he could be related to you … you two kin, Doctor?"

"Distant relatives. If you give us a moment I will call the nurses and let them take you to the floor."

"Mitchell, before he leaves, look at the energy surrounding his physical body."

I hadn't really noticed Mr. Lanauzuky's energy form. I focused as much as I could, and within a few seconds I could make out a blur of color and imagery surrounding my client. His aura was a bright yellowish-red. There were brilliant flashes of gold and silver emanating from his head. To his right, however, was a sight that I will never forget. Two teenaged boys glared at me from the haze of Mr. Lanauzuky's aura. They both seemed to be about the same age, no more than 15 or 16 years old.

Both were white males wearing cotton t-shirts and tattered blue jeans. They were barefoot. For some reason, they seemed surprised to see that I could see them. One of them flipped me the finger.

"Who are those people?" I switched to thinking mode with Djehuti. I didn't want to alarm my client with this portion of the conversation.

"They are the reason that he is ill. You see, they attached themselves to him when he stopped taking his medications. These boys died in a motor vehicle accident several years ago and they have been causing trouble since then."

"You're saying that these boys are making Mr. Lanauzuky crazy?"

"They are. Once they are removed from his form, he will fall fast asleep and wake up with no recollection of this incident. Unfortunately, the energy drain will leave him quite depressed for a time."

"How and why did they make him walk 15 miles in the dead of winter?

"They planned to use him for their own deviant pleasure. The walk was their way of extending control over his body. Debilitating his senses and tiring his higher cognitive and physical functions was part of a plan to weaken him so that they could gain long-term control. They planned to force him to accost several young women once they were able to secure adequate manipulative power over his higher thought functions."

"These guys are dead. Why aren't they somewhere going about their business in the next world? Why bother this old man?" I rejoined.

"They enjoy harassing those humans who are susceptible to their influence. This is quite a common process. They are called attaching spirits. These two boys were killed while their life force was still quite strong. As a result, they decided to remain in your world and take their pleasure from as many humans in physical form as possible. They feel completely justified in their decision. I will remove them and return them to the appropriate authorities in their world."

"How will you do that?" I really wanted to know how Djehuti would accomplish that task for sure. I was truly fascinated by the fact that what I thought to be a simple case of mental illness induced by lack of medication could turn out to be something much more complex from a spiritual energy perspective of reality.

"I will speak a Word of Power."

"You will speak one Word and poof, he's better?"

"Yes."

"Show me."

Mr. Lanauzuky had continued his trek around the room as I completed my mind-to-mind discussion with Djehuti. Just as quickly as he had taken notice of Djehuti and argued with him, he had totally forgotten that he was in the room.

Djehuti floated next to Mr. Lanauzuky and whispered something in the ears of both the boys. Their auras flared bright silver and gold. One of the boys grabbed his crotch and flipped a bony finger in my direction. Then there was a near blinding flash of light, and in an instant they were both gone.

Mr. Lanauzuky had stopped in his tracks as Djehuti approached. Djehuti then whispered another word in his right ear and Mr. Lanauzuky turned, headed straight for the chair next to the door and plopped himself down. Within seconds he was snoring—fast asleep. I couldn't believe my eyes.

"He's asleep just like that. I would have given him a sedative!"

"I am well aware of the effect of your sedatives. They only serve to dull the higher cognitive functions. This, in turn, renders the client less susceptible to conscious control from outside attachments. The would-be attaching entities then move on to the next person. You would say that the client has then recovered. This unfortunately is true only as long as they remain on medication. As soon as your patient stops his medication, he will be invaded again. You have seen this cycle manifested over and over in your practice of medicine. The only sure way to stop this cycle is to remove the offending entities and close the gate through which they entered. The first Word that I spoke to the boys sent them away from this one's body. The second Word that I spoke closed the open gate within the patient that allowed them entrance. The combined shock of closing the gate and removing the offending entities has caused him to fall asleep due to this balancing, restorative shift of energy. He will recover within a few hours and remember nothing of this incident."

"You can do this for anyone who has this problem?"

"Only those who will allow the removal. Some patients enjoy the process of being mentally ill. Others see mental illness as a just punishment for some real or imagined crime they have committed. Still others will not allow any intervention in the process of their illness. They prefer to suffer in silence. I will teach you how to remove these attachments in the appropriate cases."

Djehuti's energy form flared up in size to a brilliant silvery gold and he disappeared. Just then, Miss Johnson walked into the room.

"I see our friend is sleeping off his high, eh' doctor?"

"Yes, I suppose he is, nurse. I suppose he is. Let's get him upstairs to the Geriatric Unit Floor. I will call the orders up to them."

"Very well, sir. Will he be needing a window or an aisle seat then?"

She seemed to enjoy the banter. I guess her casual manner was a blessing tonight. Window or aisle seat was our code word for restrained or unrestrained admission to the unit. Restrained clients got the window, unrestrained clients got the aisle.

"Aisle please. But I will have them send down two aides to escort him when he wakes up, just in case." I dictated the admission summary and went on to see my next client.

As I walked the halls, I reflected upon the above event: There was a time in medicine I recalled when doctors believed that a causative agent that couldn't be seen, heard, touched, tasted, or smelled was capable of making a person ill was preposterous. Only after years of ardent research and persistence by scores of pioneering physicians did hand washing and sterile techniques become an accepted practice within the medical field. Today the study of bacterium, fungi, protozoan, and viral as well as all manner of microscopic life is a multi-billion dollar industry. No one can see bacteria with the naked eye, but they still cause illness and death on an unparalleled scale. Attaching spirits or—"lost souls"—might represent a similar unseen plague for the psychiatric community to investigate further.

Djehuti had introduced me to specific energy patterns, as yet undetected by modern medicine, that "infected" the human organism and lead to the development of mental illness. These patterns could be remnants of emotional or mental energy from a number of sources, including those persons who are no longer in the physical body. Prior to the discovery of the microscope, the Geiger counter, and X-ray technology, mankind had no way of detecting or measuring a myriad of potentially dangerous invisible health threats either. Thus I wondered if one day science might create an instrument that could measure the energies that Djehuti called attaching spirits. I of course seriously doubted that psychiatrists on a worldwide scale would ever use Words of Power during my lifetime but I, personally, would be happy to learn even one of those Words if it would help someone recover.

1:30 a.m. The next client I saw was the young girl who wouldn't talk. Adeline was a tall 17-year-old olive-skinned girl. She wore a loose brown halter-top and a very short, very tight denim skirt that barely covered her particulars. She sat on the exam table with her legs wide open. I asked Nurse Johnson to accompany me during the exam. A brief chat with her parents had revealed that Adeline was a model student and had always gotten straight A's. She had not dated much until recently when she met a young black boy named Auguste. He was Haitian. Adeline's family was Costa Rican and they had been in the US for almost ten years. Adeline's mother, a beautiful raven-haired woman who wore an immaculate royal blue Donna Karan skirt set with a matching top, provided much of the history. Her father, a somewhat older, short, stodgy white gentleman with thinning white hair stood solemnly in the corner and puffed on a Dominican cigar.

"You are the Doctor Gibson?" Adeline's mother spoke decent but slightly broken English.

"I am. Please tell me what happened to your daughter today." At this time of the night, I just wanted the facts. I had neither the time nor the energy to pursue analytical theory and investigation.

"She came home from school. Her teacher called and said she don't talk … she just stop talking like she don't hear you. She don't talk to her friends … to me … to no body. You got to help her Doctor. You are the Doctor Gibson yes? She dress funny and look how she sit … my Addy never sit like this."

Donna would look great in that outfit, I thought, as Adeline's mother talked. Her words seemed to run together after a few phrases. The only thing that kept me focused was her eyes. This lady must have been stunning when she was younger. She was still quite a lovely vision in fact.

Sadly, however, I had no idea what was wrong with her daughter.

The lab results revealed no drugs or alcohol, and her physical exam was unremarkable. Her vital signs were normal and by all impressions, she was a normal young girl. She simply didn't talk.

"I need to see your daughter now, ma'am. The nurse and I will go in with her and I will tell you something as soon as I am done evaluating her further."

"You are good Doctor, no? You will please find out why she acts like this? You will help Addy, yes?" Her mother began to cry softly and two huge tears rolled down the left side of her cheek.

"I will do what I can to find out what is wrong. Please wait outside while I talk with her."

Miss Johnson closed the door to the exam room. Adeline was totally oblivious to our presence. Spontaneous mutism was a rare symptom in a patient who had no history of any psychiatric problems. Without a history of drugs, trauma, or hysterical symptoms, I was flying blind without a rudder. This would have been an interesting case in the daytime where I could bring my full conscious faculties to bear on it. Now, at almost 2:00 a.m., after close to two days with little or no sleep, I would be lucky if I remembered how to do an interview with the girl.

Miss Johnson sat down in the corner by the door and opened an old copy of Car and Driver. She hummed the theme song to the TV show Perry Mason as I worked. I promised myself that I would accidentally step on her foot on the way out.

Instinctively, I focused my Second Sight on Adeline's aura. I half expected Djehuti to show up and help me with her care but after a few moments I realized that he would not. I was beginning to enjoy his company. Her aura colors were strange. In fact, there was only one color. Completely surrounding her form was a bright smoldering flame of silvery light. Standing immediately to her right, was this woman.

She was dark, perhaps African in extraction, rather thin, but attractive. She wore a totally white outfit that wrapped around her body like a toga. She smiled ruefully when she noted that I could see her. Then I looked closer at the girl's spiritual anatomy.

Adeline's main soul facets were completely clouded by the presence of a dark silvery film of some sort. I traced its origin back to a long threadlike cord that was connected to the lady that floated within her aura. I had a pretty good idea where her problem was coming from now. In that precise moment I heard a knock at the door. Miss Johnson opened the door and one of the nursing assistants peered into the room.

"Doctor, there is a woman here demanding to see the patient. She says she is a friend of the family." I played a hunch. If my guess was right, the woman in Adeline's aura would be the same person about to come through that door.

"Let her in please."

Within moments, a juggernaut of a woman pushed her way into the examination room. A tall thin black lady who spoke with a slightly broken English accent stood by the examination table and glared at Adeline. She wore a delicate, white cotton wrap, and leather sandals. She was the same woman that I saw in Adeline's aura.

"Where is the little whore? Where is Ms. Little Thing who thinks she can steal my Auguste?"

"Ma'am, can you tell me what is going on here?" I asked even though I had a good idea what was happening.

"She don't talk do she Doctor? Look how she dress! Look how I make her sit ... like the whore she is ... Prissy Miss! You the one who see me on her. You got the Sight? Hmmm ... a Doctor who got the Sight, Lord have mercy!" The lady's aura flared a deep silvery blue. She let out a loud belly laugh that was probably heard all the way out into the parking lot. I knew that Adeline's problem was directly connected to this person. I asked Miss Johnson to leave the room and let me speak with the lady alone.

"Yes I saw you. What did this girl do to you that causes you to ride her like this?" I was proud of myself for seeing what was really going on. Maybe there was a use for this Sight stuff. The lady had somehow fused her auric energy onto Adeline's. In effect, this allowed her to control her higher mental and physical functions. A feat like that took some skill and willpower. I had read about this type of "possession." Supposedly, it is not all that uncommon in Voodoo cultures. This lady was dangerous.

"Don't you hear nothing Mr. Magic Doctor Man? She try and take my Auguste. He is my man! She not fit for him." Adeline sat stoically and did not move a muscle. She stared blankly at the wall. I could still see the lady's image imbedded within her aura still.

"I don't want to get involved with your personal business. If this young man is yours, then this girl has no right to him. She didn't know that he was yours. I have seen her soul and she is a good person. She would not steal him if she knew he belonged to you. I would ask that you release her to my custody."

I was going out on a limb here, but I knew that this was the girl's only chance for sanity. Medical science could do nothing for her short of committing her to an asylum.

"How long you have the Sight, Magic Doctor Man?"

"A few months, enough to see some things going on with my patients very clearly."

"O.K., I will let her go. But only because you see the good in her. If I catch her with my man again I will cut out her heart. She will not get a chance to see you again Magic Doctor Man. You married pretty man?"

"I have a woman who cares for me." I didn't want to give this person even the slightest hint of an opening.

"Pity," she sighed.

With that statement she took out a large fresh cigar, lit it, and blew three puffs of smoke into Adeline's face. In seconds, Adeline shuddered and began to cough forcefully. She opened her eyes wide and looked alarmingly at the woman who had freed her. She began to cry. The woman let out a loud laugh and bolted out of the room. When I looked at Adeline's aura now, the colors had changed dramatically. Her aura was soft lavender green with blue and orange. There was no trace of the lady anywhere to be seen.

"Adeline, how are you?" She sat up straight and looked at me with those tears in her eyes still flowing freely. She was indeed beautiful like her mother.

"That woman, she was in my dream that I just had. She said awful, frightening things to me the whole time. Where is my mother?" Her voice was soft, weak; but she spoke clearly: "I want to go home."

"Your mother is waiting outside for you. Do you remember any of the events from earlier today?"

"I don't remember anything except that lady tormenting me. Are you a Doctor? Where am I? Why am I wearing these clothes?"

Adeline straightened her body and crossed her legs demurely. She tugged shyly at her halter-top in an attempt to cover herself. She seemed to be ashamed of her appearance I noted. I explained to her how she got to the hospital and why, who the woman was, and, equally, how important it was for her to stay away from Auguste. I didn't know if she believed me or not. Somehow, I felt that she did at some level.

I excused myself and asked Miss Johnson to get her parents. I didn't know what I was going to tell them, but the whole truth was not an option. Within an hour, Adeline and her family were on their way home.

I documented the case in her medical record and wrote down a diagnosis of hysterical mutism, chuckling to myself. I began to under-stand how New World explorers must have felt when they began to re-count their discoveries back home. They were sure that no one would believe the mysteries that they had uncovered as well. For certain, I knew that no one in my psychiatric department would believe what I had just witnessed. If I reported my findings just as they occurred, well, let's just say, that would not happen. I am not a martyr!

With the paperwork completed, I braced myself for my next evalu-ation. I thought about Donna and how she'd be sound asleep now. My thoughts also drifted briefly to Kathy. I liked her more than I was willing to admit then. She listened to me. That was very refreshing. I guess I hadn't had anyone really listen to me in that way in quite a long while. It felt good to be understood I chimed.

2:34 a.m. Mr. X was a very tall, very odd-looking black man. He sat up in bed eating raspberry Haagen-Dazs ice cream while sipping a 7-Up. He smiled when I entered the room. His hair was thick and matted like he had never ever used a comb. His teeth, all six of them, were in dire need of pulling. He smelled of boiled cabbages and fruit rotting on the vine. The remainder of his body was covered in a variety of stains and oily deposits that I did not care to examine. Nonetheless, I would ask Nurse Johnson to wash him thoroughly before we sent him up to the floor.

I looked at his aura but I was stunned. Within seconds I knew that something was wrong. No matter how hard I tried, I could only see his physical form. He had no detectable aura at all. Not a glimmer, not a flare-like glow of any kind: I refocused my Second Sight. I had noticed previously that the soul was suspended about one and one half to two inches behind the forehead. I had already grown accustomed to seeing it there but instead of a glowing faceted, crystalline structure, I found merely a tiny pinpoint prick of light. The faintest infinitesimal spark of light imaginable and nothing else. No matter how hard I focused, I could see nothing else whatsoever. Was this man soulless? He was the first person that I had met who had no aura and I thought this evaluation work-up ought to be fascinating—if not frightening.

"Good evening, Sir. What is your name?" He looked at me with clouded eyes. His face was at once sad and pensive. He seemed to struggle for words, and then he sat up and smiled.

"I am enjoying this body. I always wondered what it was like to be seven feet tall."

"So now you're going to tell me you're a very tall elf."

"No, I just told the constable that so I could get in here and sample some of your delicious beverages. The ice cream is splendid. Humans are very clever inventors of products."

"So, what is your name, Sir?"

"You couldn't pronounce it even if I told you. I won't be in this body long enough for that identification to matter anyway. I am just taking a look around through these sets of eyes. This human didn't need his form anymore. I will leave shortly." He sounded apologetic for something I didn't quite yet understand.

"I take it you're not human?"

"No, I'm not."

"So what are you then?"

"Let's just say I'm from a galaxy far, far, away," he wisecracked.

This conversation was very strange indeed. Tonight in general had been very strange. My Second Sight was being sharpened that much I sensed. I could see reality on an entirely different level than my colleagues. The combination of fatigue, stress, and lack of sleep had probably served to open my mind's eye. I was scheduled to graduate in a few months from this residency so this might be the last time that I would ever be on-call I said to comfort myself. Perhaps, the powers-that-be are making sure that this night shift will be uniquely instructive?

I still didn't know Mr. X's name and it didn't look like he was going to tell me anytime soon where he came from either. I wished that Djehuti was here so I could bounce these tough questions off him. I looked around the room half expecting him to appear. He didn't. I'd have to handle this perplexing case alone—as I always did prior to my contact with him.

"All I know about you is that you like expensive ice cream and 7-Up and that you were brought here naked after nearly freezing to death on the front steps of the Courthouse. If you don't start answering my questions, I am going to declare you incompetent and commit you to our unit upstairs."

He replied soberly now: "If you check the lungs in this body you will find a festering pneumonia in the right lower lobe. I believe that it is an anaerobic variety of bacteria. It should kill this form within a few hours. I will be long gone by then." His answer was almost clinical. He was totally unconcerned about my threat that was clear. But I still needed to know more about "who" or "what" he was.

"I would really like you to tell me at least a little something about you."

"If you insist, doctor. I will tell you that I am on vacation. I was floating around and saw this body lying in a near death state and I decided to hop into it. I didn't think anyone would find me but here I am. Could I trouble you for another one of these delicious beverages?"

"Vacation? From what, I mean, where?"

"I will not answer any more of your questions until you bring me more of this drink." Mr. X lay back on the bed, folded his arms, and closed his eyes in quiet protest.

This was ridiculous. I needed some air, so I left the room to get a drink for myself and Mr. X. On my way out, I instructed Miss Johnson to wash him thoroughly. She glared at me with a menacing stare. She knew that I would probably not be on-call again and that this was likely our last encounter as well. I hummed the theme song to "The Andy Griffith Show" as I walked past her. That was pure and sweet revenge!

3:28 a.m. I returned to the room and sat Mr. X's 7-Up by the bed. He appeared to be sound asleep. I shook him and he didn't budge. I touched his face and his skin was cold and clammy. My heart raced as I feared the worst. I took his pulse and my fears were confirmed. He had died. I called a Code, pushed the six-six-six emergency number on the wall phone, and began CPR. I looked around the room as I saw the tiny flicker of light hovering above the body. It slowly rose towards the ceiling, hesitated for a second, and then disappeared in a flash of light.

Despite our efforts, the medical team was unable to revive him. I looked at his body and said a silent prayer for the care of this soul no matter who he was—or wasn't.

4:41 a.m. I finished all my dictations and paperwork associated with my admissions for the night. I signed off on some special orders and headed for the call room to check messages. There was a note on the door from Kathy: I was to call her later. For the first time in many hours, I allowed myself to genuinely smile. Just then, my beeper went off. The number for the ER popped up into view again and I begrudgingly called it. Miss. Johnson was on the line:

"Hello Dr. Gibson. How are you doing this fine evening, sir?" She knew damn well how I was doing. I was exhausted. She had just seen me leave the ER dragging my tail behind me.

"I'm fine Miss Johnson. Do you have another evaluation for me?" I really didn't want to hear her answer. Morning rounds were due to start in less than three hours. With any luck, I might get a couple of hours sleep before I had to shower and change for the start of a new day.

"No Doctor. I just wanted to tell you good luck. You did a fine job down here tonight."

The phone went click and I breathed a heavy sigh of relief. A very, very long and utterly strange night had finally come to an end mercifully.

Chapter Nine
As Above So Below, As Within So Without

After my horrendous night on call, I slept for twelve straight hours. Donna and I had not spoken in over a week so I called her first thing after I woke up, but she didn't answer her phone. I debated going by her apartment, but I thought better of it. If she wanted space, I would give it to her. If she didn't want to mend our broken relationship, it was over. I would have to grieve, heal, and move on.

The difficulty with the whole moving-on process was tied to the reason we broke up in the first place. I wanted someone in my life that I could share my growing perceptions of reality. In a way, holding onto the past was a way of keeping my soul tied down to the very energies that have held me back in a myriad of lifetimes. If I was to evolve, and spiritual evolution was the foremost priority in my life, I would no doubt have to leave a lot of people that I care about behind. Initially I didn't see how difficult personal transformation could really be but I was starting to get a glimpse with every passing day now.

Ultimately I called Kathy after I decided to let Donna go. I suppose I should say, in fairness, after I accepted that I was being let go. We chatted briefly then, but our schedules had not permitted a real conversation yet. So I invited her to drive down to Baltimore with me for the day. We both had the coming weekend off and the weather seemed as though it was going to cooperate completely. Of course, I relished this opportunity to talk to Kathy about our mutual interest in metaphysics.

Speaking of which, later that same evening, I showered, dressed, and prepared for my meditative journey. I hadn't seen Djehuti since my last night on call a few weeks ago. I had even tried to visualize him and call to him in my mind, but I was unsuccessful. I wondered what he did with his days and nights.

Indeed, the events of my on-call night were still fresh in my mind. I had taken to practicing the art of examining the auras of my clients, strangers, friends, and anyone who happened to cross my path in the interim. I always found the same thing: Faces, lingering spirits, fragmented souls, geometric shapes, and aura colors in every shade imaginable were the standard fare. In fact, I had never seen the same aura color pattern twice. Everyone seemed to have an aura that was unique to them as a fingerprint, with the intensity and shading of the colors varying greatly from person to person.

I put on my meditation robe and prepared by centering myself. I completed three Breaths of Seven before I settled down into the meditative-trance mode. Soon the room faded away as my aura seemingly expanded to fill that entire space. I lifted peacefully into the air and hovered above my apartment building. The air was still with a faint scent of burning oak hanging in the breeze. I allowed myself to rise even higher into the night air.

I saw clouds of thought and prayer rising skyward from various parts of the city. Some of these bubble-like structures were light and charged with positive emotions, while others were dark and negatively charged. I noticed that the seedier parts of the city seemed to be associated with the more ominous clouds of energy. The more upscale parts of town were lit with bigger, brighter, pastel-colored cloud formations. I saw these thoughts and feelings were uplifting to all coming in contact with them and that indeed did influence the forms that took shape out of them.

The sun had just dropped below the last row of poplars that lined the streets in that part of my city. Then it occurred to me that I had never visited the Sun or any of the planets in our Solar System during my travels. I had pretty much been confined to exploring *empty space* and its exotic displays of light and dark energy.

All at once, a whole new sense of freedom took hold of me.

For I recollected that dozens of ancient cultures had worshipped the Sun as a deity. In fact, the indigenous peoples on every major continent had formed a religious cult focused on solar lords. This evening, I thought, I'd attempt a visit to our closest star and investigate it for myself. In that second, Djehuti appeared.

"I will accompany you on your journey to your Sun if you like, Mitchell." I was really glad to see him for sure.

"Where have you been? I've called you a dozen times and you haven't answered."

"I stated quite clearly that I was curious about you. I am not, however, 'obsessed' with your world. My reality encompasses a bit more of the universe that you can presently imagine."

"I didn't mean to be presumptuous; I understand that you have other interests."

"I do indeed. Before you make your present trip, I would like to prepare you for these and other upcoming experiences."

"I have a lot of questions for you," I replied. "As a matter of fact, I have a whole lot of questions that I have been saving up for you."

Our relationship had undergone a radical shift. First, I had grown to accept Djehuti's superior knowledge and wisdom. His intelligence and capabilities were far beyond anything that I would possess in this lifetime. Second, if I was to evolve, I needed to discipline, if not totally suppress, my cynical ego. It may serve us to be a "Doubting Thomas" initially but once you have your Second Sight restored that is not necessary anymore. That awful night on-call had humbled me too. I was ready and willing to listen.

"I will instruct you in certain areas that I assume have troubled you."

"I need to know what's happening to me," I cried out. "I need to know how to interpret these visions and images that stream through my mind's eye. I need you to clarify this process."

"And I will gladly serve you as a teacher, Mitchell. Let's go, therefore, to the Sun and begin our lesson."

Djehuti's form brightened to a ball-of-fire, literally. He touched my forehead and in the next moment we were floating serenely within violent tongues of flame that leaped all around us. We hovered in this realm as Djehuti spoke again:

"This is the core region of the star you know as the Sun. As you notice, surprisingly, it is calm and peaceful inside of it despite its outward explosions. Adjust your vision, Mitchell; look very closely at the surrounding scene with your newly expanded Sight. Tell me what you see."

Naturally, I had expected a blinding experience, but that is not the reality I encountered. Suspended there in this brilliance beyond description was an exact replica, albeit a bit younger, perhaps, of my own body. It was curled in the fetal position, completely nude, and unconscious. My body was composed of the same material as Djehuti was presently.

I wondered if my solar body-double here was the blueprint for my physical body on earth. As I looked deeper into this embryonic realm, I saw many more similar forms but I didn't recognize faces of the individuals. Some forms were infantile, others well-developed.

"That's me floating there. There are a lot of other people here too. They seem to be sleeping," I said matter-of-factly, as I calmed myself.

"I will explain what you are seeing from a technical standpoint. What your scientists now call quantum physics is more to this point. Something appears to emerge from virtually nothing, that they call the vacuum potential, or quantum foam, but this is reality, as you know it. Subatomic particles wink in and out of existence on a continuous basis from an underlying field of cosmic consciousness that is now known as the zero-point field. This field of infinite possibilities contains the original blueprints of creation. The Sun is a lens for the zero-point field, in other words, a quantum foam generator of life force solar energy that constructs immortal light bodies out of mortal nature."

"Your physical body is in the early stages of spiritual light body evolution. And as you continue your studies and meditations, your Light Body will awaken, mature, and replace your physical form of dense-matter with light-matter. During this replacement cycle process, it will activate the dormant DNA gene-structures within your cells and transform you into a being like myself. The development of your 'diamond self' is the goal of the Creator. Sunlight is in fact a complex carrier wave that encodes a number of energy factors that ultimately guide the growth and development of all life forms on your world. For this reason, cultures worshipped the Sun as God."

"Will all humans become light bodies at once?"

"No, there are a variety of levels of evolution that are possible for human souls to attain. Some souls remain at the lowest level of attainment during the entire course of their existence. This is usually a choice that the soul makes during its lifetime. These souls generally serve the Creator in a functionally robotic capacity. They typically choose lifetimes in which their choices are made for them and they like it that way. These souls do not wish to attain 'Radiant' status and do not work toward that end. As such, they do not possess a form represented in this star."

"There are also souls who believe in an eternal heaven or hell state that occurs after the death of the body. These souls choose to re-side in these realms until the energies used to create them are exhausted. Their essences will then be recycled having never born any physical fruit. As the human soul evolves in its awareness and knowledge of its potential, it begins to create the light body form. The dormant DNA codes are key to understanding this fact."

"Only the enlightened caterpillar knows its destiny is that of a butterfly that can float through the air with the greatest of ease. To do so, however, requires that the caterpillar change its diet in the final stages, and live in a way that prepares itself for transformation of its cocoon."

Djehuti had just answered the majority of my questions concerning the Sun, human evolution, and the manifestation of our light body, but I still had a few more:

"How long will it take to activate my light body completely?" I demanded.

"Not long."

"How long is that?"

"Longer than a while, shorter than you might suppose."

He was doing that "oracle" thing again. But I just wanted straight answers now.

"What happens to a person after they become a light body?"

"Once humans evolve to this degree of immortality, they become conscious co-creators of worlds. This idea is foreign to you at this time I know. Believe me, however, when I say to you that this is your destiny. The incessant cycle of birth, aging, death, and rebirth is unnatural in the extreme and is but a means to an end. The light body is the most natural state of being in the universe and the long-term goal."

Djehuti then touched my hand, and we left the center place of the Sun, giving me the sensation of descending through multiple layers of energy. As we dissolved, I watched my unconscious body form stir slightly and shift its position to one side. In that moment, a great twinge of anxiety and elation spiraled through me simultaneously as though I had been hit with numerous blows from a pair of tiny fists. I felt as if I might shatter like a crystal wine goblet. My physical body ached and my head throbbed as I found myself sitting on my meditation pillow dazed again from a journey into the outer reaches of inner space.

"Why do I feel so beat up?" How long were we gone?" I shouted.

"How long will I feel like this?" I knew that something had happened to my physical body. Every cell in it was on-fire, screaming that I needed rest.

"The discomfort that you sense is the result of your physical body and your light body seeking to match the same wave patterns of energy. That is, your latent DNA gene-structure is awakening, resonating, frequency-matching, weaving your two "separate" bodies together now. Information is power and so by learning these lessons you've accelerated your own evolution—and your whole species as well. For whatever one man does, he does it to all of you both the bad and the good aspects. This is why you must go and teach these lessons to others so that they will begin to understand what will be happening to them soon. Your suffering will subside within a few hours but it will come and go over time as your Sun becomes more active in the years ahead. In the meantime I will answer more of your questions, Mitchell."

"I really only have two questions and both concern that last night I had on-call at the hospital. For one, who was that 'elf' guy, the one that had no aura or soul that I could see?"

"The entity that you spoke to in the ER wasn't a created being."

"If he wasn't a created being, what was he, or it?"

"There is an entire realm of reality called the Void that predates the creation of all things. These beings are known by many names: angels, demons, elves, fairies, and so forth and now are relegated to mythology. Nonetheless, these beings are entirely real but they co-exist at a different level of energy than you do. You often see them only out of the corner of your eye because they exist at a right-angle geometrically to you. That is, they live in a parallel world that is offset—imperfectly superimposed—upon yours at that moment. When a more perfect resonant alignment occurs during optimal atmospheric conditions, such as during summer and winter solstices, you more readily detect them. That is why you find your sacred site structures on earth are designed to celebrate these seasonal events and why they are made of stone. The stones soak up the emitted and reflected celestial magnetic rays of the Sun, moon, planets—and beyond to the center "black hole" core of the Milky Way Galaxy."

"These beings cast no shadow because they are made of light-matter?" I offered.

"Precisely. They are not trapped in dense-matter."

"So that's why he wouldn't give me his name, or tell me anything about himself. You still haven't told me what manner of being inhabited that patient. Was he an elf, or what?"

"You will have trouble with the answer I am going to give you. I neglected to mention the largest entity that casts no shadow."

"Who is that?"

"The Creator casts no shadow, Mitchell."

"You mean God? That homeless guy was God? How can that be?"

"One of the greatest mistakes human beings make in the formulation of religious dogma is they place limits on the Creator and the role he personally plays in creation. As you saw, the Creator takes form at will. This was the supreme message that Jesus brought to us. He said as recorded in your scriptures: 'I am in the Father and the Father is in me. If you see me, you see the Father.'"

Those last few statements would require a lot of contemplation—ideally over a couple stiff shots of blended whiskey. I had met God, The Creator, The Big Guy himself? God drank 7-Up and hung out as a street person in downtown Philadelphia waiting for the police to bring him to an emergency room to see a psychiatrist? Say what? This was sounding like a script from the science-fiction series The Twilight Zone.

"So why didn't you come to tell me what was going on? You helped me with the others. Why not him? He was God for Christ's sake!"

"Mitchell, that was not your first encounter with The Creator. Do you remember the night when you rode a Trailway's bus back to college through the southern part of Georgia?"

"Yes, I did that plenty of times in those years."

"Do you remember talking to an elderly black gentleman on the bus in Atlanta? He sat beside you chatting away until the bus reached Albany?"

"Yes, we talked until I fell asleep and when I woke up, he was gone. I assumed that he had gotten off at one of those stops we made during the night."

"He did not get off at one of those stops. That man was God."

"So I talked to God way back then, and I didn't even know it?"

"God enjoys interacting with his creatures anonymously. In fact, everyone talks to him in person at some point during their lifetime."

"Why an old black man? Why couldn't he choose another form?"

"God can and does take any form that he chooses. In your case he simply chose a form that you would readily accept without giving it a second thought. Recall your scriptures, again, that you can even entertain angels unaware."

I could scarcely believe my ears. I had met God twice, and both times I didn't even know it. From now on, I would check everyone's body for the presence of an aura and a shadow. I vowed to myself that I would never again miss this opportunity to commune with God face-to-face.

"Why did God talk with me on those two occasions?"

"You will have to ask him that question yourself," Djehuti spoke softly.

"How do I contact God? How do I get him to come back and talk to me?"

"I might suggest that you keep your eyes open for an elderly black man who has no shadow. That seems to be his preferred persona in his contacts with you."

"I only have one question remaining. Will you teach me to use those Words of Power by which you healed Mr. Lanauzuky? I have never seen a person recover so quickly from a manic episode as I did that night. I truly want to learn that technique."

"When you recover your energies, I will reveal this lost science of soul to you."

"Thank you. I must get some sleep now," I mumbled.

Djehuti departed in a flash of light that was now a commonplace departure protocol for me to witness but I turned out the lights the old-fashioned way, snuggled deeply under my bed covers, drifting off to continue my nocturnal otherworldly life within the eternal mindscape of dreamland.

The Dream Game

Big puffs of wispy smoke drifted lazily about the dimly lit gambling hall. Nine very odd poker players nervously contemplated their hands. August, the oldest of the group and ostensibly the one with the fewest remaining molars, nervously chewed on an old tuft of Red Man. He slyly ignored the dribbling that pooled around his starched white collar. He knew that the spittle annoyed Mr. Ibis.

Two pair, Jacks high, would not hold very long, and a good bluff needed distractions. He waited for a large pool of brown spittle to build before he let it go into the porcelain coffee cup to his right. Fifteen thousand dollars would buy a lot of meat, he thought to himself. Very few people understood the intricacies of preparing a good pot of stewed rat flesh with all the trimmings. Since he had taken to eating a strict rodent diet, he had kicked his addiction to carbohydrates entirely. The tall thin man stood quietly in the corner and wondered how he could hear August's thoughts so clearly. He fidgeted nervously and tried not to be noticed by the other players at the table.

Mr. Ibis had convinced the group that Vegas Bill had no intimate knowledge of card games. Apes as a species, he argued, have an inordinate fear of gambling. Four of a kind, Kings straight, should win him enough to court the hands of several fair maidens during the coming weeks. It would also be sufficient to keep Vegas Bill swimming in Perrier through the entire winter season. Mr. Ibis looked totally out of place in his perfectly tailored, starched single-breasted gray wool suit. He had long ago traded his matching silk tie to Vegas

Bill for the ape's last Pre-Castro Cohiba. He never quite understood where Bill could get such a fine Cuban cigar without proper ID. The remaining players at the table, a sordid assortment of gangster types, cowboys, and two transvestite albino midgets, beckoned noisily for the dealer to fill their hands. They eyed the girl with taut squints and did their best to maintain the proper air of sobriety. The group got together once every year to play this game and for many it was the highlight of otherwise mundane months spent in solitude. Mr. Ibis had won the game for the last three years running. No one wanted to see a repeat of this performance. The midgets had threatened to castrate Vegas Bill and bronze his particulars if they ever confirmed the group's suspicions that he was somehow throwing the game toward Mr. Ibis.

The tall thin man in the corner walked slowly around the table and glanced uneasily at each of the player's hands. He stopped briefly to examine August's cards. He moved along quickly after he caught the broad end of the draft that August released into the room. It smelled of oranges and rotting rat flesh. Why someone would stick to a diet as horrible as his was well beyond the thin man's understanding. For a moment, I felt sorry for the man and wondered why he even bothered to remain in the room. Before I finished the thought, Mr. Ibis lifted from his chair and walked directly in front of the thin man. He plucked an ice cube from his glass of Scotch and held it out to him. The thin man looked with a long vacant stare and slowly held out his right hand to receive the ice. August suddenly came out of his chair and pushed Mr. Ibis forward with his hand.

"You old bastard, I know you are trying some stuff with this young fella here. By God, if I catch you cheatin, I'll gut you myself." August pressed his two pair close to his chest and warily eyed the rest of the group to see if they had tried to sneak a peak at his cards.

"Leave him alone!" The room grew deathly silent. The thin man had shouted at the top of his lungs and looked as if he were prepared to back his words up with action. Mr. Ibis straightened himself and fixed his gaze squarely on the thin man's eyes.

"Who are you, sir? Tell us your name." The thin man seemed totally taken aback. The full contingent of players surrounded him and began to repeat Mr. Ibis' question in unison. I thought to my-

self what a weird dream. Then I realized that I was wide-awake, but still dreaming.

"We did it! We did it! We did it!" The entire party of players danced around the table and reached up to slap the thin man on the back. I pulled back and looked at the group.

In an instant, I sat straight up in bed. I looked down at my right hand and I saw a square-shaped reddened area that felt oddly cold to the touch. I realized that I had been dreaming. I remembered the entire scene and the incident with Mr. Ibis. I had yet to figure out how the cold sensation from the ice cube in the dream had presented itself to my waking state. I glanced at the clock near my bedside and realized that I had been sleeping for perhaps four hours. Before I could let myself analyze the situation any further, my eyelids grew heavy and I fell into one of the deepest sleeps that I had had in years.

Chapter Ten
Science of Soul

The last several weeks had been surreal. Perhaps stress is the catalyst for opening us to the latent powers resident within our DNA's subconscious mind? Whatever the case, once the window opened between Djehuti and my mind's eye, my learning curve shifted into high gear. The mystery to the life, death, and rebirth cycle and the overall scheme of evolution now made sense completely: We are becoming fifth-dimensional light beings.

And the more I used my Second Sight to learn about the world, the more I wanted to learn about it. Each new day brought me closer to understanding mysteries that had baffled centuries of seekers. Though I was nowhere near answering all my questions, I had come to the joyful understanding that I finally had the proper meditative skills for further exploration, as a number of patterns became abundantly clear.

First, I had learned more about the soul and the universe in the last few months than I had in my entire life. Djehuti had opened my Second Sight to a degree that I had never experienced previously. His interactions with me flowed with purpose and meaning. He wanted me to grow. I could feel it.

Second, a large part of the learning process centered upon accelerating the unification of my body and soul. I came to understand that the visionary experiences and lucid dreams that I now experienced almost nightly were slowly dismantling my old way of thinking and feeling. My old self was all but dead.

The persistent pressure that interpreting my interactions with Djehuti created, the deepening of my insights that I gained from my awakened Second Sight, destroyed my ego's self-focus. My worldview had become more holographic; I was beginning to see space (and time) more organically, holistically, as a living being in which I was embedded. I was a child of the cosmos and I knew it now.

The past, present, and future is a tapestry woven out of whole cloth—not the haphazard patchwork quilt that religion or science envisioned it was hundreds of years ago.

The death of my old self brought with it the most important key to real growth: It was being true to one's self. The loved ones in my life would have to learn to accept me for who I genuinely am deep inside myself, not the artificial facade; the persona they had projected onto me from their own desires to control people that believed different from them.

A visionary experience like mine changes a person. Initially, I felt as though I were split in two, living a double life. The world, I realized, was unconscious. Each day we walk blindly through our days as pro-grammed robots and experience one day pretty much like the day before. Experiences outside of the norm were denied, feared, and filed away as meaningless anomalies. Ironically, many times, these paranormal experi-ences are the most defining moments in our lives. Yet, we don't speak about them publicly?

Thankfully, I had been given the blessing of awareness, the power of observation from an early age—as have many people studying this emerging science of soul. Thus, as much as I tried to explain away my spiritual side employing physical laws, it simply grew stronger through synchronistic happenings as it was supposed to do to get my undivided attention ultimately.

Moreover, all my hard work and preparation to become a practic-ing psychiatrist was about to come to fruition. I had not told anyone about Djehuti but I knew that I needed to if I were to resume a balanced lifestyle. Kathy was the perfect candidate and I loved how easily I could talk with her. Her presence in my life at this particular time was a major blessing. She was born in California into a large Baptist family. Her fa-ther had been a minister for many years before he developed a fatal kid-ney illness. Her mother was a schoolteacher and a consummate preacher's wife that could handle these pressure cooker environments.

Much of Kathy's strength came from the foundation established by these two wonderful, loving human beings that gave her life. She had been an All-American track star and basketball player in high school and college. Despite her rather conservative upbringing, she had managed to retain a remarkably open mind I soon discovered. In her case, she began to question her traditionalist teachings after her first powerful visionary experience three years ago. While she was praying during one of her fa-ther's sermons, she saw a glowing white form materialize above the choir. The form that resembled a woman with chiseled features came closer and hovered near her for several minutes and then floated quietly through the roof of the church. She didn't notify her family about her vision then either.

But after we met, she told me later, she felt that for the first time she was able to openly talk about her experience. To my surprise, she even admitted that she had experienced two such visitations following her first encounter. She was as happy to finally share her experience with me as I was mine with her. Our conservative backgrounds and comparable mystical experiences led to communications that were sincerely rewarding to both of us. The fact that she was beautiful and extremely intelligent simply added icing to the already scrumptious cake.

This relationship had promise I saw from that moment onwards. I loved her laugh and smile in particular. Even though we had barely just met, I dreaded the thought of never seeing her again as I was moving to Arizona after I finished my residency. I had received several good job offers from hospital firms around the country. However, more than anything else, I wanted to live in a warm desert climate. Arizona had spoken to me in a way that few places ever had previously. Three thousand miles separated Philadelphia from Phoenix. Good relationships, especially those that feed the mind, body and soul, are rare and precious commodities to obtain. If I were going to make this one work, I would have to give some serious thought as to how we would stay geographically connected. My intention was to not let this gal get too far away from my side.

After we had been going out for about two months, Kathy and I sat down and talked for a couple hours about everything that surfaced: life, death, ice cream, but most of all, Djehuti. For the first time in a long time, I felt secure enough to candidly share my myriad experiences with him. She went home that night contented I sensed but called me rather startled shortly thereafter. She said that she felt a presence in her bedroom. She was unable to see anything, but the feeling was unmistakable. I offered a reasonable explanation for the phenomenon and that seemed to work—or so I thought. Thus I completed my evening meditation, showered, and went to bed. However, a few hours later, at 1:17 a.m, my phone rang. Kathy's voice pierced the silence like a siren:

"I saw something. I don't know what it was. I don't know even how to tell you."

"Just tell me. Take a deep breath, focus, and get it out," I counseled.

"He floated ... this large, really bright man just floated into my bedroom ... and he was looking at me."

"What was it Kathy?" I asked as I started to throw on my clothes.

"It was a person ...but people don't float, Mitch ...do they?"

Only hours before, I had told Kathy about Djehuti, and of course I wondered if he had decided to visit her but I wanted to stay objective. I realized that I had no real control over his travels in our world and if he had indeed materialized in her bedroom, as he had mine, then that would certainly explain her fear at the moment.

"Kathy, I think Djehuti visited you."

"Why do you think that? You said he was beautiful and peaceful. He woke me up out of a sound sleep and scared the hell out of me. I didn't invite him here."

"We've been talking about our visions and meditations. Perhaps he is listening?"

She was silent for a long moment. I knew she was collecting her thoughts and I sensed her energy field was stabilizing.

"Let's call him Mitch, right now. I have to know ... this sort of thing doesn't happen to me as often as it happens to you. I want to see for myself."

Her response was heartening. She was a brave woman. I admired that about her.

"Let's do it then Kathy. I'll be over in a few minutes."

"No, Mitch. I want to call him right now ... I want to see him appear right now ... I need this, Mitch, for me!"

"Alright, we'll call him right now." Kathy was exercising her need to exert some control over the situation. Intense visionary experiences tend to have that effect on a person; I knew that feeling for control in these situations only too well.

"Let's focus together. Bring your awareness to a calm still place and focus on his name. Repeat it clearly in your mind over and over. I'll do the same."

"I hope this works Mitch ... I have to know the truth."

"It will work, Kathy—trust me. If I'm right, he wants you to know."

For a few brief moments we focused together. I envisioned Djehuti as clearly and vividly as I could possibly do. After a few minutes, I felt a shift in my consciousness. Moments later, I knew that we had made contact.

"He's here Mitch! I see him! I see him!"

"Tell me what you see." I was as excited as she was now. For the first time, I was sharing a spiritual vision with another human being at the precise moment it was happening.

"He's gold, shiny looking ...he looks ... just like you said ... tall ... bigger than I thought and he's just floating there not saying anything ... this is so cool ... I can see him!"

Kathy's mood changed from fear to excitement. I sensed Djehuti's presence within my mind, but I could not see him.

"He's going away ... he's fading, Mitch ... I can't see him anymore ... make him come back ... please, I want to talk to him now."

"Kathy, I think he just wanted to say hello. I don't control his actions. I think his appearance was more of a courtesy than anything else."

"I believed you Mitch but I didn't know for myself—now I do. I was scared, but I'm not anymore. I feel closer to you now." Her words were sweet music to my tired ears.

Djehuti wanted to remove doubt about this whole thing with me I mused to myself.

"He is real, just like you said. He's a real person." I could hear the giddiness in her voice as her tension melted away. Mine melted as well.

We talked on the phone most of that night about God, the universe, visions, mythology, meditation, and everything else even remotely related to our epiphany. By morning I was exhausted, but relieved. We had shared an experience that would bind us forever. From this night on, I knew that I would always share my life, at least to some extent, with this woman.

The following morning I rose, showered, and headed straight to work. Even though I had only slept a couple of hours, I felt rested and relaxed. Sharing Djehuti with Kathy had lifted a tremendous burden from my spirit and hers as well I imagined.

Still, a heavy haunting sensation began to cloud my senses. It began in the pit of my stomach and gradually inched its way north into my skull as the morning wore on. I had become accustomed to these omens over the years. Invariably, they serve as a warning. Every time I have felt this foreboding, something ominous happens in my life. The sensation never gives me specifics as to the exact nature of the problem. The only guidance that I seemed to receive from these early warning signals was indicated by their intensity; the bigger the feeling, the larger the problem to manifest. I was five years old when I first experienced this sensation.

At that time I tried to ignore it but within an hour of its appearance, my youngest brother had made up his mind that he was going to dive headfirst into a five foot tall red ant hill that had formed in the field near our home. He was two years old at the time. I was the first to find him. Luckily, I was able to rescue him before he had been bitten too extensively. For my trouble, I received some particularly vicious bites on my upper thigh and knee. I still carry those scars today. From all indications, whatever I was to face that day was destined to be a problem of tremendous proportion.

The morning passed without any significant stressful event. I began to think that perhaps, for once, the sensation might be a false alarm. My beeper went off at 2:16 p.m. My hopes were immediately dashed to pieces.

I received a call from the surgical post-operative ward to see a woman who had recently attempted suicide. She had tried to kill herself by shooting herself in the chest with a .38 caliber pistol. Luckily, the bullet only pierced the tip of her left ventricle and exited through the lower lobe of her left lung. Her boyfriend had found her within seconds of the blast. He placed his finger into her heart to stop the bleeding. With his other hand he dialed 911.

His efforts saved her life.

Her injuries were repaired surgically and her vital signs were now stable. As far as the surgeons were concerned, her medical care was now the Department of Psychiatry's problem. The Charge Nurse was glad to see me.

"Dr. Gibson. I hope you are feeling your oats this morning. This lovely lady, Miss Sarah Hoffman, is ready for transfer to your floor." Hilary Griffin was a raven-haired older nurse who had been working at Albert Einstein Medical Center for over 30 years. She had been born and raised in the Ardmore region of Philadelphia. She was heir to a rather large real estate fortune. She worked as a nurse because she loved caring for those less fortunate than herself. She was truly a gem. I had answered many emergency calls during her shift, and yet I had never seen this particular look on her face. She looked nervous, almost to the point of being frightened. Her aura flashed a dull reddish-orange and white. Something was spooking her and that was for certain.

"What's wrong Hilary? I read Miss Hoffman's chart. The case seems fairly straightforward. She's lucky to be alive."

"She wants to sign out of the hospital against medical advice Doctor." The reddish-orange colors in Hilary's aura deepened and expanded slightly in size. I looked briefly down the hall toward the patient's room. I saw a hazy silvery glow that emanated from the doorway to her room.

"She's not going anywhere. If she tries to sign out against medical advice, I will have to get an emergency 302 order." A 302 was an order issued by a court that would allow me to admit the patient against her will. I needed the signature of at least one other physician and the phone approval of a Judge. We only used them in serious cases when the patient was a clear risk to themselves and others. Someone who had just tried to put a bullet through their heart was not going to get a second chance today.

"I told her about the 302. She told me if you or anybody else tried to commit her they were going to be sorry. We put a nurse in with her until you could get here. She's a scary one, Doctor. Be careful."

My gut radar kicked into overdrive. I was glad that someone would be in the room with me while I interviewed this client. A violent, suicidal, and resistant patient could be a very dangerous person indeed.

I was not about to take any chances with her. I glanced through her chart and made my way to her room. As I approached her bedside, the air grew thicker and warmer. A gray aura-like haze congealed into a soup-like fog that hung sickeningly over the client's bed now.

Sarah Hoffman was an angry soul. She sat straight up on the hospital bed and glared defiantly at me as I stepped closer. She was in her early twenties, but she looked much older. Her eyes had a slight yellow cast that spoke volumes about how she had spent her days and nights. The sallow complexion of her cheeks and the sunken hollow space around her temples told me that she was probably in very poor health. I shuddered to think of what she had endured during her young life thus far. She was five feet five inches tall. Her muscles were well-defined, and she looked as though she might have been an athlete at some point.

"What the hell do you want, Doctor?" In my young years as a physician, those words almost never bode well for a good relationship with a patient, especially upon a first meeting.

"Miss Hoffman, I am here to evaluate you. I am a psychiatrist from the Seventh Floor. I read about what happened to you. I think we can help you feel better about yourself so you won't try this again."

"Look here, I don't want your help! I just want to go home so I can get this damn thing done right! I will not miss this time!"

Her aura thickened and rolled forth like angry thunderheads cooked-up by the heat of a summer Sun. She stared hard at me and yelled at the top of her lungs. I knew that my best Marcus Welby, M.D., bedside mannerisms would be wasted on this lady. She was determined to kill herself, violently. She was dangerous.

"Miss Hoffman, I can't permit you to leave this hospital and try to harm yourself again. I believe that you are suffering from a life-threatening mental illness that needs to be treated. Do you really want to try to kill yourself again after all you have been through?"

"Get out of here Doctor! I'm leaving here and NOBODY is gonna stop me!"

"Sarah, let's be reasonable. I just want to get a good history on you so we can get to the bottom of why you want to do these things to yourself. I want you to calm down and talk to me for a few minutes. I'm here to help you. I will not let anyone hurt you."

"GET THE HELL OUT OF MY ROOM! I DON'T WANT YOU HERE!"

Sarah's aura flared bright silvery red. She stood up on her bed and swung at me with her gaunt fists. I backed away and began to leave the room. As I moved away, I saw two large, red, darkly luminous forms pierce the fog of her expanding aura. They moved and roiled in the center of the fog like twin rain squalls battling for control of an evening storm. They moved toward me with frightening speed. Before they could penetrate my aura, Djehuti materialized and absorbed their energies in a dazzling flash of gold light. He then vanished just as quickly as he appeared. I dashed out of the room and made my way to the nurse's station. Within seconds, I heard a loud crash coming from Sarah's room and over my right shoulder I saw her running down the hall after me. She had pulled all the lines out of her chest and arms and she was trailing a curious mixture of saline, blood, urine, and electrical cable leads. She was yelling obscenities at the top of her lungs.

"CODE 5! CODE 5! CODE 5!"
"FIFTH FLOOR SURGICAL SUITE ...
FIFTH FLOOR SURGICAL SUITE!"

Hilary had placed a Code 5 call over the PA system. A Code 5 was an emergency call to the Psychiatric Emergency Response Team. They were on-call during the day shift for these types of emergencies. The hospital budget cuts had erased their much-needed services from the evening and night shifts, unfortunately.

Sarah ran straight toward me. With one violent swipe, she knocked over all of the charts, computers, and nursing monitors from the counter. Before I could blink twice, she had grabbed an IV pole and swung it toward my head. I ducked and moved back away from her. Two large male nurse's aides grabbed her and tried to hold her back. Two nurses jumped in front of me and shielded me with their bodies. A third aide came barreling down the hall with a straight jacket in hand. I wished that Djehuti had given me those Words that he used on Mr. Lanauzuky. I could use them now.

"HALDOL 10MG IM STAT! ... BENADRYL 50MG IM STAT!"

I yelled a quick set of orders to the staff. Haldol and Benadryl in those doses would quickly calm her down. She had just made my task of securing a 302 much simpler.

Hilary administered the medications that I prescribed, and within minutes, Sarah was sedated and safely strapped into a gurney for transport to the PACU. For the first time all day, I breathed easily as I felt this was the crisis I had been bracing myself.

"Thank you, Hilary. Thank all of you for helping with this lady. You saved my neck."

"I had a bad feeling about her, Doctor. I was ready to call a Code the moment you went in there."

"How did you know, Hilary?" I wondered what had cued her in to the danger that Sarah presented.

"I don't know, Doctor. Sometimes, you just know." Hilary began the task of cleaning up the mess that Sarah had made for her.

I called my attending supervisor and filled him in on what happened. He was supportive of my decision to 302 Sarah. He was glad that I wasn't hurt in the process. So was I of course as I finished the paperwork and left the unit. I wondered why Djehuti had chosen to appear and disappear so rapidly. For some strange reason, I wanted to see Sarah again as soon as possible. I didn't know why, but I felt unfinished business where she was concerned.

On the other hand, she was still a dangerously disturbed and suicidal person who was not currently under my care. Still, I felt drawn to her. I knew the resident on duty in the PACU and I convinced him to let me talk with Sarah for a few minutes. She had been placed under heavy sedation since her transfer and she also had been constrained further by arm and leg restraints. She could not physically harm me in any way.

I stood by her bedside and stared at her sleeping face. Her aura was still quite disturbed although the sedation blurred the angry coloration. She looked almost peaceful as she slumbered. I stood there at her bedside for a few minutes before I felt it. A short, stabbing pain rocked my forehead backwards and caused nausea and dizziness before it then subsided as quickly as it came over me. I stepped back from the hospital bed and headed for the door. Before I could reach the door, Djehuti appeared.

"Mitchell, the discomfort you are experiencing has been caused by your interaction with this woman." Djehuti's energy seemed brighter than usual.

"What do you mean?" I was puzzled by his remark and, to a certain extent, by his sudden appearing and disappearing acts too.

"We haven't much time. I will explain as we go. You must come with me." Djehuti touched my forehead and within seconds I was out of my body. I noticed that he had placed a bright lavender blue covering or sheath over my still form. I had never seen him do that before.

"What's going on? Why the rush?" We began to move swiftly and in the blink of an eye we were attending Sarah's aura and looking into her soul energy patterns. It didn't take long for me to see why she was so sick.

"This woman is suffering from a variety of serious mental maladies. She is far beyond your power to help her because the source of the disturbance is within her etheric field of energy. Nevertheless, she has caused you great harm."

"How? What has she done to hurt me?" I knew that something was wrong by now.

"Do you recall when you administered energy to her when you were attempting to convince her to cooperate with you?"

"Yes, I do. I projected gold and white light in an attempt to calm her down."

"Where do you think the energy of that light emanated from, Mitchell?"

"I don't know. I thought I was giving her mental energy or something like that."

"The energy that you chose to give her emanated from your soul material. The reason that you feel the pain and discomfort in your being is related to the fact that Sarah now carries within her a number of your soul facets. You gave them to her of your own free will, Mitchell."

An involuntary shudder rippled through me.

Now I understood my need to see her again. I had made a grave mistake in judgment without realizing what I was doing. As I peered into her soul, instead of facets that were crystal-clear and energetic projections, I saw a ghastly-disfigured structure that was severely damaged.

From all appearances, her facets looked as though they had been ripped away by some massive explosive force. The structure that remained reminded me of pictures that I had seen of a mountain after a large volcanic eruption had blown away much of its surface. The life force energy emanating from her soul's gem was weak and evanescent. It was a dying ember, literally. I could easily see the gray and black force that surrounded her aura and leaked from her facets. I was instantly attracted to them.

"So that's why I needed to come back to see her. At some level, I knew that something was wrong. What's so bad about her having a few of my fragments? If they will help her get better she can have them, or so I had thought."

"At one level, your sentiments are noble. But you made a serious mistake by allowing her to obtain possession of your essence in that manner. Her soul is in a rapid state of decay. Many healers in your world make the same mistake. In an attempt to help those in need, they give of themselves in a similar fashion without even knowing it. As a result, they willingly give away facets of their own soul structure and find themselves "burned out" as caregivers way too soon. This gift has a steep price."

"The recipient unknowingly accepts this energy but invariably it is not enough to repair the damage and shift the field into balance, as is the case in this patient. The fragments of your soul that you gave her will be consumed to no avail. In return, you will begin to experience headaches, fatigue, and a variety of emotional disturbances as long as your soul essence remains in the vicinity of her decaying soul force field. Unless there is a concerted effort to "retrieve your soul" you will feel depleted to a certain degree. For this reason, many people who work with serious mental illness, violent criminals, and severe trauma victims often become ill themselves. Souls in a critical state of decay will often seek out those who will give them the energies that they need to forestall their own self-destruction."

"Why is her soul in this condition? What happened to her?"

"Before I answer your question, consciously will your soul fragments that you see in Sarah back into yourself. They will automatically adhere to their proper positions within your soul structure facets as they have your unique magnetic signature."

I mentally gathered my glittering soul fragments and instinctively pressed them to my abdomen's solar plexus region. I estimated that I had "given" her about a dozen soul fragments. I saw two large shimmering orbs approach me as we prepared to leave. They reminded me of the red and black forms that Djehuti had intercepted earlier. They grew in size as they raced towards us. As they approached, they trailed a loud crackling noise that reminded me the sound fire makes as it rages through a burning building. Djehuti took my hand and whisked me out of Sarah's body aura before the orbs could reach us. I looked around and realized that I was back inside my physical body right where I began this soul journey process again.

"What's going on here? What are those things? Why do they keep coming after me?"

"There are many things in your world that are not of your world. They belong to the worlds that exist between ours. In order to understand Sarah's disturbances, you must understand what she has been through naturally. This woman was physically, psychologically, and emotionally abused by those that loved her for years. She ran away from home when she was 15 years old and learned very quickly that in order to support herself she would need to master certain trades. Among other things, she became a prostitute, thief, and cocaine addict. She married one of her customers when she was 18 and soon became pregnant. When her former pimp found her and discovered that she was pregnant, he beat her with a broom handle. He then brutally raped her. He threw her down a flight of stairs and left her to die. Her husband found her and took her to the hospital. She lost the child, and unfortunately, she has not seen her husband since. After she was released from the hospital, she moved into a halfway house and tried to clean up her life."

"Her pimp found her again and convinced her to go back to work for him. That is when her depression set in. She could not perform her duties well and he beat her often. The more he beat her, the more depressed she became. She ran away from him and came to Philadelphia to start her life over. She met her present boyfriend and took a job in a small bookstore. She never received adequate treatment for her depression and as a result, she came to your attention after a suicide attempt."

"Trauma of this nature will often cause the loss of soul facets. Street drugs, poor nutrition, disease, and a series of unhealthy living environments have contributed to the creation of strong destructive energies that now threaten to consume her. These unbalanced forces of nature are a beacon to a variety of beings that would feed upon this soul. As a soul decays and falls into increasingly greater levels of depravity, there are beings who would seek to further this process for their own survival ends. They would feed on this energy as a source of food as any other parasite would do. Indeed this situation is not unlike that of an opportunistic viral infection. Life is solar light in all its many biological, chemical, and electromagnetic forms—and it has no preference. Human beings are in that sense experiments in the survival of cosmic consciousness on your planet."

"What are those orb things and how do you know so much about Sarah?" I asked next. Djehuti seemed to know a lot about Sarah. As a matter of fact, he seemed to know a lot about a lot of the clients that were in my charge. His recounting of her history answered a lot of questions. It had also raised quite a few as well. I understood now why Sarah had become so despondent and suicidal. I also understood why her soul was in its current state. I even understood why I had been drawn back to her side. My headache and nausea had subsided and I felt refreshed thanks to the reunion of my soul fragments with their rightful owner. I still didn't understand what those two orbs were and why they kept attacking me.

As if on cue, Djehuti responded: "When Sarah's child died, it attached itself to her soul essence. The child could not accept that the body had died, and therefore it sought to continue its life inside Sarah's body. A child does not realize that it has died and becomes an attaching spirit floating within Sarah's soul pattern field of energy. This soul is one of the forms that tried to attack you. After years of witnessing attacks on its mother, the child has become quite protective. He attacked you out of instinct. The child was to be born a boy."

"The second orb is that of Sarah's former pimp. Because he raped her, he willfully injected a portion of his soul essence into her being, just as a form of branding or marking does for lower animals. He attacked you because he believes that you are a threat to his property. The two attaching spirit forms act together out of instincts for survival of their energetic food source, not as a result of any conscious coordinated effort.

Your species, we say in the higher realms, will prey upon one another until you learn to pray for one another!"

"Thank you for your help with Sarah. But, Djehuti, please tell me how do you know so much about my clients?"

"As I have said, you and I are of the same soul lineage—or grouping of soul skills. You are the physical aspect of my higher being, as are many others currently in this world performing similar tasks for God. It works like fractal geometry: just like two snowflakes are part of the same family, yet no two snowflakes are exactly alike either. We truly are facets of one another, in other words. In medicine, you are assigned to the physical care of a patient and all the subsets of functioning (emotional, mental, etc.) that pertains now. I am assigned to the same clients at the higher dimensions of reality to care for their soul needs long-term. In essence, I am taking care of the same people that you are, only in a different way. When our purposes cross paths, I will help you with them. Such is the case with Sarah."

Djehuti helped me to understand our relationship in a much deeper sense than I had ever thought possible as a physician. His explanation made perfect sense as I was connecting the dots between realms at a faster pace. All beings existed multi-dimensionally, so it was as above, so below, as within so without. I guess souls need doctors at all levels of existence just as much as we need them here and maybe this soul medicine training and learning program never ends either? It was an intriguing idea to contemplate.

"So what can we do for Sarah? Do we just leave her like this?" I glanced at the clock overhead. I had been in the room over 45 minutes and I needed to move on with my rounds.

"Sarah will need to actively participate in her recovery process. If she chooses, she may elicit the aid of her Spirit in her healing. All she need do is ask, and the necessary energies will be given to her."

"You mean she can fix all the damage to her soul by just asking her Spirit to come in and make it all better?"

"In many ways, it is that simple. To be sure, this is a challenging situation for this soul to face but in truth there are simply positive and negative energies. She would have to be shown the necessity of performing positive thinking to offset a lifetime of negative life experiences and she would have to believe in such things, and she does not, as you have seen, before she will benefit. Unfortunately, this is not as simple as it sounds because human beings are addicted to their pain and suffering because your beliefs become your biology. This is why Words of Power in fact work at the level of the soul. I look forward to revealing more on this topic in our mutually-shared lucid dream space tonight. That is a much more productive state of mind as the mental noise of this world is so loud that it is oftentimes counterproductive to learning the science of soul wisdom teachings."

Djehuti then vanished. I recalled that in all the commotion over Sarah, I had forgotten to ask him why he had chosen to visit Kathy. I also wanted to know why I was becoming lucid within my dream-states so frequently. I was starting to put more of the pieces of the puzzle to the game of life together in terms of physics and metaphysics now and this was satisfying indeed. I finished my rounds for the day, finally, and left the hospital. I had seen as much as I could take of the Psychiatric Ward for one day.

Upon returning home, I treated myself to a long leisurely bath before dinner. The last two days had been grueling. I had not slept more than six hours total. Tonight, I would sleep like a log I promised myself but only after a brief meditation. Djehuti had promised to give me the Words of Power this evening, and I needed to clear my mind. After I had completed three cycles of the Breath of Seven, I could no longer keep my eyes open. I glanced at the clock on my dresser and noted the time: 10:45 p.m. I was exhausted, yet I called Kathy to say goodnight and within minutes was in bed fast asleep.

The Words of Power Dream

I awoke within a large cavern. As I moved around, I noticed that my feet were stepping on what felt like large pebbles. I looked down at the floor and saw perfectly cut faceted emeralds. Some were pebble-sized; others were the size of lemons. I picked one up and stared at it for a few moments. It was a deep velvety green and larger than a baseball. I looked up and realized that the ceiling and walls of the cave was covered with these stones as well. At that moment, I knew that I was dreaming and I became lucid in it.

A bright flash of light filled the chamber and for a split second I couldn't see anything at all now. But when I recovered my vision, the chamber was no longer empty. In the center of it, where there was once only an empty space, there now stood a large raised stone structure. The material that formed the base looked like obsidian or black marble and had a rectangular platform on its surface. This platform was covered in a substance that was neither silver nor gold, but contained properties of each. Resting upon the platform was the biggest book that I had ever seen.

As I approached the platform for a closer look, Mr. Ibis and Vegas Bill flashed into view. Mr. Ibis wore a deep navy blue tuxedo with matching Gianfranco Ferre alligator shoes. Vegas Bill wore only a black New York Yankees baseball cap. He was puffing on one of his expensive Cuban cigars, again. A few seconds later, Vegas Bill disappeared and Mr. Ibis was left alone, as the scene morphed simultaneously and the familiar golden floating form of Djehuti hovered before us.

"I made you a promise Mitchell, and I intend to keep it. I want you to learn continuity. It is important for you to relieve yourself of the prison of your limited acceptance of reality. The real you is alive in dreams and beyond. It is time that you became more active in these realms. For this purpose, I have guided the awakening of your dream body self."

"Where are we?"

"You now stand within a very sacred place to me. It is within these walls that I store the 'pearls of great price,' the total sum of your world's magical dreaming formulations. I want you to see this, Mitchell. Approach."

I approached the Book with reverence. The closer I got to the book, the bigger it got. Its cover smelled like fine leather and was unmarked except for a geometric symbol that I had never seen before. Yet the symbol seemed somehow strangely familiar. It glowed with a soft luminous light that conveyed that it was alive. The Book was over three feet thick and conscious because it contained the Words of Power.

"Mitchell, when you are ready, I want you to open the pages of the Book and gaze upon any portion that you wish. You may view as much or as little as you desire. I caution you, however; if you choose to open the book and look upon its pages, you will be changed forever."

"Changed how?" I had learned a lesson earlier that day. "Can it harm me?"

"The Book contains far more than knowledge. It also contains Words within its pages that when spoken have the Power to heal souls. Such power is not easily absorbed by human beings at this time, physically or psychologically, and others have suffered ill consequences from choosing to use them unwisely."

"What happened to the others?"

"An unfortunate few have been unable to preserve their sanity. The viewing is your choice, Mitchell; the consequences of that viewing are not. Therefore choose wisely."

Before me stood the secrets of the ages. One of the greatest Egyptian deities of all time had brought me to his inner sanctum in order to keep a promise. If I chose to look upon the pages of the Book and learn how to speak these Words of Power, I risked insanity if I could not manage them properly. I wished that I had more time to ponder the choice but I trusted Djehuti implicitly. He had intervened on my behalf on more than one occasion. He had become a guide, teacher, and friend to me. I knew with every fiber of my being that he would not allow any harm to come to me.

"Turn to the middle portion of the Book and gaze directly at the symbol you see."

I used both hands to open the book. As I looked at the first page before me, the symbols leaped into my brain with a living fire. The images and shapes ignited like lightning bolts zigzagging through my eyes. I could feel this raw energy move past my optic nerves and settle into my neurological network. The back of my head began to grow hot and my brain cells throbbed under the pressure. I touched the letters with my fingertips, and the energy filled my whole body with rivulets of electricity and heat. I heard celestial music, symphonies, melodies, technically perfect chords of violin and vocal pieces played to full completion in seconds. I wept from the sheer joy of it all.

Then I saw paintings that danced upon writhing canvases. The colors and textures of the pigments dazzled my inner vision with their radiance and complexity. I touched one of the geometric shapes *within one of the paintings, and the image began to sing to me. I did not recognize the language, but the words and music were so beautiful that I thought my heart would burst. The song evoked soul-filled memories of the first time that I hugged my mother in public, my beloved grandmother's kiss upon my cheek as a child, even my recent conversation with Kathy. I drew my hand away from the symbol before the emotions and images overwhelmed me totally. I looked down at my body and I saw that it was glowing. My entire being had become infused with a white light luminosity that pulsed through every cell within my body. I forced myself to turn another page.*

A robed figure sat alone shivering in a cave. He was old, perhaps one hundred years by human reckoning. His robe was a beautiful olive green and blue material that looked like silk. He stared at me vacantly and turned slowly to look toward the ceiling of the cave. A vivid white light sprang from his forehead and illuminated the darkness of the dwelling. After a few seconds, the light completely enveloped the old man. His entire body glowed with an exquisite inner luminescence that lit-up the entire cave complex. He turned his gaze back to me and smiled: I turned another page.

A small group of children stood floating above the abyss of a tall cliff. As they floated, they chanted a prayer that sounded something like Japanese. Their faces beamed as I watched them. One of the children whispered the words of the prayer into my left ear and vanished as quickly as she appeared. The children disappeared into the horizon. I turned the page again.

The next set of symbols immediately adjacent to this image seemed to have a much lower energy content than the preceding forms. I touched these nine symbols and immediately was transported to a place of incredible power. I tried to focus my sight, but the intensity of the light was far too strong. It was as though I was trying to stare directly into the heart of the Sun. For a moment, I thought I could make out a few human shapes milling about in the distance. But just as quickly as they appeared, they were gone. The place was permeated by a thunderous booming sound that deafened me. I withdrew my fingers from these symbols, closed the Book, and stepped away from the platform exhausted. I understood why Djehuti had given me the warning; I was not ready to receive too much of this power at once.

Djehuti hovered in front of the Book. He was smiling.

"That was beautiful," I said.

"You have prepared yourself well. I merely showed you the way."

"I feel different. I am in my dream body, but I feel even more alive and awake than when I am in my physical body. My head is full of so much stuff—powerful, moving images. What do I do with all this information?"

"You will know what to do with it when the time comes."

"I think I'm good for a while," I replied graciously. "Thank you."

"Mitchell, you have your second sight; you need to use it in service to your fellow beings now."

A small sphere of blue light materialized above Djehuti's head and I, instinctively, looked into it. My heart started to race and I could feel the urgency that surrounded the images I was viewing.

"Is this true? Is this vision really going to happen?" I probed.

"The images that you witness are in the process of manifesting into your world as reality. If you do not personally intervene in them, it will transpire just as you have foreseen. That choice to take action—or not—is yours to make, Mitchell."

I saw a terrible event. Somebody close to me was in grave danger. I willed my consciousness back into my physical form.

Chapter Eleven

IN SERVICE OF THE SOUL

1:39 p.m. The Sun was streaming brightly through my bedroom window. I sat up with a start and looked at the clock on my dresser. My body had slept for 15 hours even if "I" had been elsewhere. I grabbed the phone and called the PACU.

"I need to speak with the nurse in charge." Randy, the daytime supervisor for weekends, answered the phone. He was surprised to hear my voice.

"Dr. Gibson, why are you calling today, sir? You're not on-call."

"I know, Randy. Who is the Charge Nurse today?"

"I am today. Bert called in sick and I'm covering. What do you need, Doctor?"

"Randy, has Sarah had any visitors today?"

"I don't know; let me check the log. Hold on Dr. Gibson." I could hear him rustling through some papers. As he spoke, I was busily throwing on my hospital scrubs and resident's coat.

"Yes, her brother from New York is here visiting her now. Is there something wrong Dr. Gibson?"

"Randy, Sarah is an only child. She doesn't have a brother. Get in there and check on her right now. I think she's in danger. Call the intern and get him to the unit STAT. I'll be right over."

I hung up the phone, grabbed my car keys, and bolted for the door. My gut instinct radar had just kicked into high alert—DANGER—mode. I ran three red stoplights on my way to the hospital. I arrived on the PACU within minutes. The place was in utter turmoil. Two armed Philadelphia policemen stood guarding the entrance to the main doors to the PACU Crisis room. I flashed my medical ID badge and the policemen stepped aside. Sarah's room was filled with a variety of uniformed personnel. Several patients from the unit were standing nearby trying to see what all the fuss was about. I waded past the cacophony of bodies and peered over the side of the bed to get a look at what was going on. Overhead, the hospital PA system blasted an alarm:

"CODE 3 PACU! ... CODE 3 PACU!"

Sarah had been shot in the head and was dying.

She lay still in the bed and her aura flickered with the mass of colors that were streaming out of her physical body into her spiritual body that had begun to gather in the corner of the room now. I could clearly make out her face and shoulders as they coalesced into soul energy forms. This unfolding scene was just as I had viewed it within the sphere of blue light only hours before.

I knew who had killed her and so did the police.

Whitfield Gainey was a short, fat, balding Puerto Rican man with no visible teeth in his head and he was handcuffed to the victim's bed railing. He was quite a sight to behold wearing a bright yellow three-piece suit with a wide-brimmed hat. White patent leather shoes matched his white vinyl leather coat and both were heavily splattered with blood. He looked up at me and threw a broad toothless grin. Our eyes met and suddenly I understood Sarah's hate for this man. His beady, glaring eyes reminded me of a reptile. I stared at him for a few long tortuous seconds. His aura was a malevolent mixture of green and black and I watched as sparks leaped from the center of his forehead attaching themselves to the policemen nearby.

Without second-guessing my authority to do so, I spoke a Word of Power. I watched as a shaft of light sprang from my lips and seared its way into the soul energy of Whitney Gainey. Within seconds, his aura brightened as if sunlight had penetrated him and he glared at me with a long piercing stare. I smiled softly in return. I had finished my work with this man. He would not harm anyone else again in this lifetime.

I glanced at Sarah. She had totally left her physical form and her soul had completely re-integrated in the corner. The medical team called off the Code 3, and she was pronounced dead. The PACU staff, Intern, and Charge Nurse were speaking to the police and detective assigned to this case. I headed down the hallway to exit the floor. But before I got outside the main door, Randy stopped me with a touch on the shoulder.

"How did you know, Dr. Gibson? You called in out of the blue like you knew something was wrong!"

"I had a bad dream last night and Sarah was in it. My nightmares sometimes come true, Randy, what can I say? It's a gift—or is it a curse?" I mused.

Randy stood there staring at me. I couldn't think of anything else to tell him, and he couldn't think of anything else to ask. So I punched in the release code and walked out of the PACU. Even though I couldn't save a "physical" life that day, perhaps I could help spiritually.

I locked the call room door and turned off the lights. To do what needed to be done, I would only need an hour or so alone. I climbed onto the double bed and began to calm myself. By the third iteration of my Breath of Seven protocols, I felt myself shifting consciousness and out-of-body ready to go to work within this realm now.

This time I had a mission: My goal was to search for Sarah's soul body.

I knew that she would be confused from the violent death that she had just endured. Ironically, however, I recalled that this is just what she had wanted for herself in the first place. The only difference was that she had someone else do the dirty work for her I had to imagine. Although hospitals are very strange places in and of themselves with people coming and going at all hours of the day and night, I was shocked to see what happens to some of these unfortunate souls that "passed" away in these facilities.

They didn't leave them—or at least not soon enough!

The first person that I encountered was an elderly white man who stood in the recreation room watching television. He had no shadow and his aura was almost transparent. When he noticed that I could see him, he walked toward me, passing directly through a lounge chair that sat in front of him. I really didn't have time to talk with him, but he wasn't taking no for an answer.

"You can see me can't you, son? Help me. I need to find my daughter so she can take me home. I can't get anybody here to listen to me. I want to go home." Robert Tankar had suffered a massive heart attack and died in the ICU more than three weeks ago. He didn't know that. So how do you break that kind of news to someone? You are "dead" but not really, really dead? I grimaced as I recalled similar double-talk in the *Wizard of Oz*.

"Sir," I replied gently, "I have to see another patient right now, but as soon as I am finished with her, I will come back and talk with you."

"This is a damn poor system if you ask me. I pay good money to get medical care in this place and nobody even takes the time to spend five minutes with me." Mr. Tankar returned to his spot in front of the television set watching the news. Two elderly women walked through him on their way to the restroom. He didn't notice them.

Mr. Tankar was not the only lost soul I encountered this day. There were literally dozens of dearly departed ones wandering up and down the halls of the hospital. One elderly black lady floated idly near the water cooler on the sixth floor post-surgical suite. She had suffered from a bowel obstruction that had perforated and spilled infected fecal matter into her abdomen. She died within hours of her admission, despite some rather heroic medical interventions I recalled. But Ethel Robinson's mortal frame had passed from this world two years ago! I made a mental note to try and help her later.

Fifty-one-year-old Glen Tatum had suffered a fatal stroke six nights ago. He sat in the waiting area of the hospital lobby naked from the waist down, enjoying a raucous conversation with two young women who had died in a fire. They ignored me when I asked if they had seen a soul matching Sarah's description.

I continued my search inside and outside the hospital grounds.

Seven-year-old Tommy Sanders had been killed when he fell down a flight of stairs. He had been playing Superman with his brother David, who had wanted to see if Tommy could really fly while wearing the new cape with magical powers. Tommy was actually flying for a moment—until his head hit the third step on the stairway. He now sat in front of the hospital on the grass by the sparkling water fountain waiting for his mom to pick him up. His body had been cremated two months ago and he really looked lost. I would see him right after I found Sarah I promised.

Finally, I spotted Sarah as she was walking past the hospital dining room. I willed my form toward hers. Her aura flashed a bright array of silvery green and red. I deduced that the newly dead might still carry vestiges of their former life energies for a time. She was walking rather briskly with intention. I touched her lightly on the shoulder. She spun around and swung at me with a vicious roundhouse right. I ducked and backed away quickly. This was not going to be easy I could see. Even in death, some things never change I realized.

"Who do you think you are touching me? Back off!" She paused, stared at me for a second, and then just as unexpectedly burst into tears. I could still plainly see the gaping hole in her temple that Whitfield's bullet had created.

"Sarah, I am very sorry that this tragedy has happened to you. I am here to help you."

"Help me do what? I'm dead! You can't help me do nothing. But I know what I am going to do. I'll make damn sure he gets his reward!"

I was afraid of that outcome: Sarah wanted to exact revenge on Whitfield Gainey. That was understandable, but in my vision I could see that she intended to attach to his heart muscle and kill him slowly. The incipient narrowing of the inside of his main descending coronary vessel would make her task that much easier. But she did not realize that by attaching herself to his body, focusing her life force energy, she would be doomed to living another lifetime with this man as a major player in it. This was a habit of hers, I saw, and she needed to learn the lesson of forgiveness if she wanted to be free from her mental illness.

"Sarah, you're making a big mistake. This thing that you want to do is wrong. It will only make things worse."

"How do you know? What is worse than this? He shot me?" Her tears came in wide torrents. I felt truly sorry for her. I hoped her cathartic emotional release would ease some of her anger. The fact that she knew that she had passed over was certainly an encouraging sign. That would make my job a little easier.

"He did shoot you. You did die. He was your pimp wasn't he?"

"Yeah, so what Sherlock? He's going to be right here with me in a few."

"Sarah, aren't you curious as to how I can see you?"

"It is obvious that you see dead people doctor!"

"I see many things, Sarah. If you sit with me, I will explain the best I can."

Two police officers rushed past without noticing us. One officer did give a slight shudder like he'd been hit by a blast of cold air. Sarah lowered her head and walked slowly toward me. She placed her right hand over the wound in her temple and began to grieve, sobbing softly. I felt this woman's distress.

I spoke a Word of Power. I directed a radiant blue energy toward her wounded head. Within seconds she was encased within a bluish white light. The wound closed and healed instantly then. Sarah looked at me and gave me a wry half-smile.

"That's some cool trick you got there. How did you do that? My head is better?"

"I used a Word of Healing."

"Just like that. You didn't have to touch me or nothing?"

"That's right."

Sarah walked through the wall next to the elevator and entered into a small classroom. I followed her and sat down in a chair by her side. She looked up at me and then looked away.

"Why do you want to help me anyway? I ain't done nothing but try to hurt you?"

"Sarah, I am sensing that I have been your doctor for a long, long time; perhaps several lifetimes in fact. I have recalled a memory that the last time I took care of you, you and your child died in childbirth. Ever since then, you have been angry with me and so we meet again. You blamed me for your pain and loss of life. But there was no way that I could save you then. In that life, Whitfield had thrown you from a moving wagon when you were eight months pregnant trying to abort it. Your injuries were far too extensive for your body to heal itself. You waited for him to come back to this world again as well as me to even-the-score. Yet you forgot all about your plan for revenge and fell in love with him, just like you did previously. That is, you began this lifetime right where you left off last lifetime. There are no coincidences; we are all part of each other's soul energy equation based upon the Law of Attraction. What you resist will persist until it is resolved peacefully without a magnetic charge placed upon it. And you will keep repeating this dysfunctional cycle of 'what goes around comes around' until something happens within you to change it."

I spoke another Word of Power and the lifetime series of events that I described to Sarah verbally now displayed themselves visually to her consciousness in vivid, holographic clarity. This was the type of telepathy that I had learned mankind is evolving towards in the 21st century. Our next step up the multi-dimensional ladder is, in fact, as Professor Leonora Leet, Ph.D. at St. John's University in New York reveals in *The Secret Doctrine of the Kabbalah: Recovering the Key to Hebraic Sacred Science*. "From the fifth dimension on we may see the highly developed soul capable of synthesizing the atomic constituents of material particles [out of consciousness]." Sarah watched the images that I had projected for her until I sensed her discomfort was getting too intense at seeing so many, many lifetimes of making bad relationship choices and the results they manifested for everyone.

"You can stop this?" she whimpered.

"Sarah you can stop this if you choose. But if you go back and attach yourself to him energetically and begin the cycle all over, there is nothing I can do for you except stay out of your way next lifetime."

Sarah closed her eyes and sighed heavily. Her form began to shake and vibrate spasmodically. Without warning, she let out a piercing wail that shook me to my core. I saw Tommy Sanders, Glen Tatum, and the two ladies who had perished in the fire come running. They stopped and peered through the doorway. They gazed at Sarah for a moment and at me, and then drifted away. Sarah straightened her shoulders, and walked over to the window, staring into the sunlight filtering through the partially open metal blinds. She went silent as her aura turned a pearly blue and white pastel mixture of color. All shades of gray dissolved.

"Sarah, you can go to the Light. You can leave this place and find peace."

"I don't want Light! I want to live. I want a life. I want to be happy and live like everybody else. Is that so wrong doctor?"

In that moment, Djehuti appeared. He hovered over Sarah and touched her softly on the forehead. Surprisingly, she didn't seem startled.

"Hey, I know you. I saw you when I was a little girl. You're David, my guardian angel!"

"I am here to help you Sarah. It is good to see you again."

Djehuti floated away from Sarah and stopped in front of me.

"I am here to help you Mitchell."

"What should we do? Sarah does not want to go to the Light."

"Let's go to work."

Djehuti now touched me on the forehead and I sensed that he was creating a matrix, a deeper web-like connection of light waves between us three. Seconds later we were all three standing in the hospital obstetrics delivery room. Amy Chen, a young Chinese woman, lay writhing in the stirrups. She was in the throes of labor. I could easily make out the child's head. From the readings on the monitor nearby, however, I could tell that child was in trouble as Djehuti confirmed my concerns telepathically only seconds later.

He spoke to my mind: "This woman is due to deliver a child within minutes but the body has yet to choose a soul. As you can see, Mitchell, the monitors indicate that the mother will live but the infant will be still-born unless we intervene. Sarah, if you wish, you may claim this form. It is your choice."

"What do you mean? You mean I can just take over this body and I'm alive again?"

Djehuti looked at her and smiled.

"Yes, Sarah. The child's parents are good people. You will not be abused nor mistreated by their hand. They will take good care of you. They will see to it that you will grow up to be healthy and happy." Djehuti beckoned her to come closer to the mother. Amy Chen let out a loud scream and pushed the baby's shoulders through the birth canal. Sarah walked closer to the woman and looked at the struggling body before her. Amy Chen was 28 years old and a beautiful woman.

Her husband, Ralph Chen, a successful architect in Central Philadelphia, waited anxiously in the Father's room. This was their first child. Djehuti spoke a Word of Power and showed Sarah a glimpse of the child's future. Sarah smiled and turned to both of us. As she turned, the baby's body fully delivered. There was no heartbeat and the child's color

was dark blue and gray, slipping away fast. Then the child did not move.
     "Sarah, if you are to claim this form, you must do it now."

     Djehuti's voice was firm. The medical staff erupted into furious action. They were working frantically to save this child. Amy Chen lay back on the bed and panted air in exhausted gulps.

     Sarah walked over to the infant, kissed it tenderly and disappeared within it in a burst of light. The child coughed and spit up a thick mucous substance all over its chest. It took a deep breath and let out a loud ear-piercing cry. The nurses burst into tears of joy and great relief as the baby's skin turned a lively shade of reddish-pink and began to wiggle around on the blanket. I turned to Djehuti and we both looked at the mother. Ralph and Amy Chen were the proud parents of a healthy baby boy. With any luck, Sarah's nightmare as well as my own was over—at least in this case.

Summary

Kathy and I married after I finished my residency.

We moved to Arizona to explore the latest alternative "energy medicine" treatment modalities in fact. After all my experiences with Djehuti, I hoped to become a healer that could walk that thin line between the old and the new healing protocols, too, and I sensed that there was an openness to change the closer one got to California!

Occasionally I would hear Djehuti's voice in a dream but I had not seen him during my meditations. My experience with the Book had given me new insights into the workings of the worlds both here and hereafter. I suppose Djehuti was giving me time to digest and assimilate all the material that I had absorbed. I was thankful to him for that certainly. Up until now I had told no one about the overwhelming experience in the cave—except Kathy. However, I sense that writing about even that today is becoming almost commonplace for laymen as well as scientists. So many folks are having these otherworldly encounters.

Physicist Claude Swanson, Ph.D., has come to the same exact conclusions as I have regarding the death-like dreaming states of trance. He writes in his new text *The Synchronized Universe: New Science of the Paranormal*, "Entering deep meditation states causes a synchronization of the vibrations of the DNA in the body, and it is very likely that this is one of the keys to 'psychic superpowers.' ... 'Phase' acts like a fifth dimension which distinguished one parallel reality, one 'universe' from another." The fifth dimension is experienced every time we phase shift between Earth (unconsciousness) and Heaven (consciousness). Again, "earth" is symbolic of dense-matter physical energy, and "heaven" is symbolic of subtle light-matter spiritual energy.

Although these flamboyant claims may seem too fantastic, I can tell you today without a doubt whatsoever that they are true spiritually and scientifically. They have in fact already been verified in the laboratory by Russian scientists as documented in the report issued on January 17, 2005 titled "Russian DNA Discoveries Explain Human Paranormal Events." I shall briefly summarize what is given in detail in the book "Vernetzte Intelligenz" by Grazyna Fosar and Franz Bludorf. The book unfortunately is only available in the German language at this time. Here are the main points of their paradigm-shattering discoveries that validate my own conclusions based upon my life experiences as a medical doctor:

- Esoteric and spiritual teachers have known for ages that our body is programmable by language, words, and thought. This has now been scientifically proven and explained.

- The human DNA is a biological Internet and superior in many aspects to the artificial one. The latest Russian scientific research explains phenomena such as clairvoyance, intuition, spontaneous and remote acts of healing, self healing, affirmation techniques, unusual light/auras around people (namely spiritual masters), and the mind's influence on weather patterns and much more.

- In addition, there is evidence for a whole new type of medicine in which DNA can be influenced and reprogrammed by words and frequencies WITHOUT cutting out and replacing single genes. Only 10% of our DNA is being used for building proteins. It is this subset of DNA that is of interest to western researchers and is being examined and categorized. The other 90% of the information is considered to be worthless, or "junk DNA."

- The Russian researchers, however, convinced that nature was not dumb, joined linguists and geneticists in a venture to explore that 90% of "junk DNA." Their results, findings and conclusions are simply revolutionary!

- According to there findings, our DNA is not only responsible for the construction of our body but also serves as data storage and communication. The Russian linguists found that the genetic code—especially in the apparent "useless" 90%—follows the same rules as all our human languages.

- To this end they compared the rules of syntax (the way in which words are put together to form phrases and sentences), semantics (the study of meaning in language forms) and the basic rules of grammar. They found that alkaline-pairs of our DNA follow a regular grammar and do have set rules just like our languages. Therefore, human languages did not appear coincidentally but are a reflection of our inherent DNA.

- The Russian biophysicist and molecular biologist Pjotr Garjajev and his colleagues also explored the vibrational behavior of DNA. In brief the bottom line was: "Living chromosomes function just like a holographic computer using endogenous DNA laser radiation." This means that they managed, for example, to modulate certain frequency patterns (sound) onto a laser-like ray that influenced DNA frequency and thus the genetic information itself.

- Since the basic structure of DNA-alkaline pairs and of language is of the same structure, no DNA decoding is necessary. One can simply use words and sentences of the human language! This, too, was experimentally proven!

- Living DNA substance (in living tissue, not in vitro) will always react to language—modulated laser rays and even to radio waves, if the proper frequencies (sound) are being used. This finally and scientifically explains why affirmations, hypnosis and the like can have such strong effects on humans and their bodies. It is entirely normal and natural for our DNA to react to language.

- While western researchers cut single genes from DNA strands and insert them elsewhere, the Russians enthusiastically created devices that influence cellular metabolism through modulated radio and light frequencies, thus repairing genetic defects.

- They even captured information patterns of a particular DNA and transmitted it onto another, thus reprogramming cells to another genome. So they successfully transformed, for example, frog embryos to salamander embryos simply by transmitting the DNA information patterns! This way the entire information was transmitted without any of the side effects or disharmonies encountered when cutting out and re-introducing single genes from the DNA.

- Of course the frequency has to be correct. And this is why everybody is not equally successful or can do it with always the same strength. The individual person must work on the inner processes and development in order to establish a conscious communication with the DNA. But the higher developed an individual's consciousness is, the less need is there for any type of mechanical interface device: one can achieve these results by oneself. Science will finally have to stop laughing at such ideas and will confirm and explain the results. And it doesn't end there.

- The Russian scientists also found out that our DNA can cause disturbing patterns in a vacuum, thus producing magnetized wormholes! Wormholes are the microscopic equivalents of the so-called Einstein-Rosen bridges in the vicinity of black holes (left by burned-out stars).

- These are tunnel connections between entirely different areas in the universe through which information can be transmitted outside of space and time. The DNA attracts these bits of information and passes them on to our consciousness. This process of hyper-communication (telepathy, channeling) is most effective in a state of relaxation.

- Stress, worry, or hyperactive intellect prevents successful hyper-communication or the information will be totally distorted and useless. In nature, hyper-communication has been successfully applied for millions of years. The organized flow of life in insects proves this dramatically. Modern man knows it only on a much more subtle level as "intuition." But we, too, can regain full use of it.

- As an example from nature, when a queen ant is separated from her colony, the remaining worker ants will continue building fervently according to plan. However, if the queen is killed, all work in the colony stops. No ant will know what to do. Apparently, the queen transmits the "building plans" even if far away—via the group consciousness with her subjects. She can be as far away as she wants, as long as she is alive.

- In humans, hyper-communication is most often encountered when one suddenly gains access to information that is outside one's knowledge base. Such hyper-communication is then experienced as inspiration or intuition (also in trance channeling). The Italian composer Giuseppe Tartini, for instance, dreamt one night that a devil sat at his bedside playing the violin. The next morning Tartini was able to note down the piece exactly from memory. He called it the Devil's Trill Sonata.

- For years, a 42-year-old male nurse dreamt of a situation in which he was hooked up to a kind of knowledge CD-ROM. Verifiable knowledge from all imaginable fields was then transmitted to him that he was able to recall in the morning. There was such a flood of information that it seemed a whole encyclopedia was transmitted at night. The majorities of facts were outside his personal knowledge base and reached technical details of which he knew absolutely nothing. When hyper-communication occurs, one can observe in the DNA, as well as in the human, supernatural phenomena.

- The Russian scientists irradiated DNA samples with laser light. On screen, a typical wave pattern was formed. When they removed the DNA sample the wave pattern did not disappear, it remained. Many controlled experiments showed that the pattern continued to come from the removed sample, whose energy field apparently remained behind. This effect is now called phantom DNA effect. It is surmised that energy from outside of space and time still flows through the activated wormholes after the DNA was removed. The side effects encountered most often in hyper-communication in humans are inexplicable electromagnetic fields in the vicinity of the persons concerned.

- Electronic devices like CD players and the like can be irritated and cease to function for hours. When the electromagnetic field slowly dissipates, the devices function normally again. Many healers and psychics know this effect from their work: the better the atmosphere and energy, the more frustrating it can be for recording devices as they stop functioning at that exact moment. Often by next morning all is back to normal. Perhaps this is reassuring to read for many, as it has nothing to do with them being technically inept. It means they are good at hyper-communication.

- Now that we are fairly stable in our individual consciousness, we can create a new form of group consciousness—namely one in which we attain access to all information via our DNA without being forced or remotely controlled about what to do with that information. We now know that just as we use the Internet, our DNA can feed proper data into the network, can retrieve data from the network, and can establish contact with other participants in the network. Remote healing, telepathy, or "remote sensing" about the state of another can thus be explained. Some animals know from afar when their owners plan to return home. This can be freshly interpreted and explained via the concepts of group consciousness and hyper-communication.

- Any collective consciousness cannot be sensibly used over any period of time without a distinctive individuality; otherwise we would revert to a primitive herd instinct that is easily manipulated. Hyper-communication in the new millennium means something quite different.

- Researchers think that if humans with full individuality would regain group consciousness, they would have a god-like power to create, alter and shape things on Earth! And humanity is collectively moving toward such a group consciousness of the new kind.

- Fifty percent of children will become a problem as soon as they go to school, since the system lumps everyone together and demands adjustment. But the individuality of today's children is so

strong that they refuse this adjustment and resist giving up their idiosyncrasies in the most diverse ways.

- At the same time more and more clairvoyant children are born. Something in those children is striving more towards the group consciousness of the new kind, and it can no longer be suppressed.

- As a rule, weather for example is rather difficult to influence by a single individual. But it may be influenced by group consciousness (nothing new about this to some indigenous tribes). Weather is strongly influenced by Earth resonance frequencies (Schumann frequencies). But those same frequencies are also produced in our brains, and when many people synchronize their thinking or when individuals (spiritual masters, for instance) focus their thoughts in a laser-like fashion, then it is not at all surprising that they can influence the weather.

- A modern day civilization that develops group consciousness would have neither environmental problems nor scarcity of energy: for if it were to use such mental powers as a unified civilization, it would have control of the energies of its home planet as a natural consequence.

- When a great number of people become unified with higher intention as in meditating on peace—potentials of violence also dissolve.

- Apparently, DNA is also an organic superconductor that can work at normal body temperature, as opposed to artificial superconductors that require extremely low temperatures to function. In addition, all superconductors are able to store light and thus information.

- There is another phenomenon linked to DNA and wormholes. Normally, these super-small wormholes are highly unstable and are maintained only for the tiniest fractions of a second. Under certain conditions stable wormholes can organize themselves, which then form distinctive vacuum domains in which for example, gravity can transform into electricity.

- Many spiritual teachers also produce such visible balls or columns of light in deep meditation or during energy work, which trigger decidedly pleasant feelings and do not cause any harm. Apparently this is also dependent on some inner order, quality and origin of the vacuum domain. There are some spiritual teachers, like the young Englishman Ananda, for example, with whom nothing is seen at first, but when one tries to take a photograph while they sit and speak or meditate in hyper-communication, one gets only a picture of a white cloud on a chair.

• In certain Earth healing projects, such light effects also appear on photographs. Simply put, this phenomena has to do with gravity and anti-gravity forces that are ever more stable forms of worm-holes and displays of hyper-communication with energies from outside our time and space structure. Earlier generations that ex-perienced such hyper-communication and visible vacuum domains were convinced that an angel had appeared before them: and we cannot be too sure to what forms of consciousness we can get ac-cess when using hyper-communication. Official science also knows of gravity anomalies on Earth that contribute to the formation of vacuum domains. Recently gravity anomalies have been found in Rocca di Papa, south of Rome, Italy.

Truthfully, what we do to one, we do to all of us through the hyper-communications and transmutations of our whole human family's one-in-the-same microscopic DNA macromolecule. Anthropologist Jeremy Narby reminds his readers in The Cosmic Serpent: DNA and the Origins of Knowledge: "DNA is approximately 120 times narrower than the smallest wavelength of visible light." That means our physical body is made of cells of light that is "invisible" to our physical eyes by which they were made: Think about that a moment. This is a deep mystery. French priest Pierre Teilhard de Chardin understood the significance of this revelation when he said that our human body is nothing more than our "spirit moving slow enough to be seen." Some learned people are even saying that this speaks to what the planet is doing through the changes in her vibrations that those geometric tattoos called crop circles are revealing to all those who have eyes—the wisdom—to see it.

That to me is the ultimate message embedded within the symbols of the Book of Revelation too. The SUN behind our Sun, that the Mayans and Egyptians knew was the "black hole" energies within the core of the Milky Way Galaxy, is pulling our electromagnetic north-south polar axis to a new angle alignment in order to stimulate the opening of our third eye via the cleansing of our seven major chakras—our vortex-like centers of consciousness. That is, we want to allow the Light of God to flow through us unimpeded now that we may become one light-matter body being again. Wes Marrin, Ph.D. confirms in *Universal Water*: "In both ancient myths and modern premises, vortices are commonly recognized as vehicles for connect-ing different worlds, whereby vastly different energies encountered in otherwise distinct realms are able to converge in the space-time phenomenon of a vortex."

In summary, I am still coming to grips with all the changes that Djehuti created in my life. I do know, however, that I am a better man today because I faced the mysteries of my living soul with him as my guide than had I gone it alone. Interestingly, as I apply my new found skills to my growing psychiatric practice, I find most people have no desire whatsoever to hear about the spiritual causes of their mental health problems. For those people, 90%, I practice a very conservative brand of medicine that meets their needs. But for the remaining few, 10%, those few who are open to exploring the inner spiritual worlds with me, I have seen miraculous sometimes spontaneous healing take place. Therefore, my passion in life remains helping all those souls that present themselves to me, wisely employing what I see as the emerging science of soul in the 21st Century.

About the Author

Dr. Mitchell Earl Gibson is a board-certified forensic psychiatrist, author, and public speaker. He received his medical degree from the University of North Carolina at Chapel Hill, completing his residency training at the Albert Einstein Medical Center in Philadelphia. During his last year of residency, Dr. Gibson served as Chief Resident in Psychiatry and received the Albert Einstein Foundation Research Award for his work in Sleep Disorders. He is a former Chief of Staff at the East Valley Camelback Hospital in Mesa Arizona and a Clinical Professor of Medicine and Psychiatry at the Midwestern College of Medicine.

Dr. Gibson has been listed among the Top Doctors in Arizona in Phoenix magazine on several occasions. He has also twice been named to the Woodward and White listing of the "Best Doctors in America". In 2003, 2004, and 2005 he was honored with listings in the Consumer Research Council of America's compilation of the Top Psychiatrists. He is a Diplomat of the American Board of Psychiatry and Neurology, the American College of Forensic Medicine, and the American Board of Forensic Examiners.

Dr. Gibson is the author of Signs of Psychic and Spiritual Ability, Signs of Mental Illness, The Miracle Prayer, and Releasement. His works have been listed under Outstanding Discoveries by Kirkus Reviews, The Psychology Today Book of the Month, and Outstanding Authors by BookReviewClub.com.

Dr. Gibson has worked as a mental health consultant for Forest Pharmaceuticals, Smith, Kline, and Beecham, Bristol Myers Squibb, Intel, Samaritan Health Services, Essence, Upscale, Ebony, and First for Women, and The Arizona Republic. He also served as mental health consultant for Channel 12 in Phoenix AZ for more than eight years. Dr. Gibson has lectured extensively throughout the United States, Canada, and Europe as a noted public speaker on various topics including creating mental health without medication, the spiritual causes of mental illness, human potential, the mind-body-spirit connection, and creativity enhancement.

Dr. Gibson teaches a spiritual development course and conducts seminars on the topics presented in this book.

Contact information:
Mitchell Earl Gibson, M.D.
1577-D New Garden Road
Suite 295
Greensboro, NC 27410

Email: charbelmaklouf@aol.com
Website: www.tybro.com

Printed in the United Kingdom
by Lightning Source UK Ltd.
133195UK00002B/247-249/A